CW00762245

THE
EMERALD TABLETS
OF
THOTH-THE-ATLANTEAN

TRANSLATED BY DOREAL
A LITERAL TRANSLATION OF ONE OF THE MOST
ANCIENT AND SECRET OF THE GREAT WORKS OF
THE ANCIENT WISDOM TOGETHER WITH "AN
INTERPRETATION OF THE EMERALD TABLETS"

BY DR. DOREAL

IN ADDITION

* TWO TABLETS NOT PRINTED PREVIOUSLY *

* FACSIMILE OF ORIGINAL TABLET'S COVER *

* MAP OF ATLANTIS *

* THREE ARTICLES ON ATLANTIS BY DOREAL *
SECRETS OF ATLANTIS
ATLANTIS AND LEMURIA
ATLANTIS AND ITS PART IN THE NEW AGE

Copyright 2002

All Rights Reserved.

No part of this publication may be reproduced, stored in a retrieval system, or transmitted, in any form or by any means, electronic, mechanical, photocopying, recording, or otherwise, without the written permission of the author.

BROTHERHOOD OF THE WHITE TEMPLE, INC.
7830 OAK WAY
SEDALIA, COLORADO 80135 U.S.A.

Published by Dog Ear Publishing
4010 W. 86th Street, Ste H
Indianapolis, IN 46268
www.dogearpublishing.net

ISBN: 1-59858-242-9

This book is printed on acid-free paper.

Printed in the United States of America

TABLE OF CONTENTS

INTERPRETATION OF THE EMERALD TABLETS

INTRODUCTION

THE BROTHERHOOD OF THE WHITE TEMPLE— ITS ESTABLISHMENT AND PURPOSE

In the central United States, amidst the foothills of the Rocky Mountains of Colorado, is located the World Headquarters of the Brotherhood of the White Temple, Inc., Corresponding Metaphysical College and Church. This Esoteric School is the repository of the Ancient Wisdom. These Great Teachings of Light and Harmony, once hidden and shrouded in secrecy, are now brought to light and made available to the world to those who walk the Path of Light and Truth.

The Brotherhood of the White Temple is dedicated to the perpetuation of the philosophy and Teachings of the Great White Lodge as brought forth and disseminated by its Founder, Dr. M. Doreal. Dr. Doreal established this Organization as a means whereby Truth could be given to the people of earth.

DR. M. DOREAL, SUPREME VOICE

Dr. M. Doreal, by the following Proclamation given at the beginning of his Ministry on earth, attested to the fact that he was an instrument of the Great White Lodge.

PROCLAMATION

"Be it known to all men that I, the mouthpiece or Voice of

the Elder Brothers, speak with the authority of the Great White Lodge.

I am instructed by the Council of Twelve to make known to the world certain of the laws of the Brotherhood of the White Temple.

For the first time in many centuries, the Great White Lodge is prepared to give fully of their knowledge to those who are seeking the Path of Light.

Now, to the head of the Council of the White Lodge, I turn over all of the work I have done previously. The preparatory work is finished, and we now come under the full direction of the Great White Lodge, henceforward all responsibility rests upon the Council. I shall give as they direct, and withhold as they direct; my voice will be the voice of the Council for I have been given authority to proclaim their teachings.

All development will be under the direction of certain brothers of the Temple who will work invisible to man. These brothers shall, from time to time, be present at the convocations of the Temples, and for this purpose there shall be two chairs reserved, placed according to the ritual, and never occupied by any material body.

It has been promised that we will be aided in every way, consistent with the aims and purposes of the Great White Lodge.

Supreme authority remains with the Great White Lodge, and all changes in form, ritual and ceremony will be subject to their decree.

I, as Supreme Voice of the Brotherhood, acknowledge my

obligation to the Great Council of the White Lodge, knowing that only through their aid will TRUTH become universal."

In the Threefold Light,
Doreal—F.G.W.L.
Supreme Voice

THE GREAT WHITE LODGE

`The Great White Lodge' so often referred to in occult literature, is only a legend to the average student, nevertheless it exists. `Shamballa' is the name most often used in referring to the Central Headquarters of the Great White Lodge. Its location has never been definitely known to any except the Adepts and their Chelas, though it is usually believed to be in some hidden valley in Tibet, though not on the surface of the earth, for it is located in a great space, hollowed from the very heart of the Himalayas.

There are 144 members of the White Lodge, all men or women who have attained full Illumination and are in At-One-Ment with the purpose and plans of the Universal Mind. Each of these 144 have ten chelas making 1,440, who in turn have ten lesser chelas making 14,400. Each of the 14,400 work in various ways through ten others who are not chelas, but are high in development having passed certain initiations. Thus we have in the outer world the mystic number 144,000 which is so significant to students of symbolism.

The Brotherhood of the White Temple has a direct connection with the Great White Lodge, and at all times works under their authority. All teachings and principles are under their jurisdiction. We are proud to acknowledge our submission in all things to the Highest Constituted Authority of the planet, for in their hands lies the future growth and development of man.

ILLUMINATION

The ultimate goal of all phases of the Brotherhood of the White Temple's Teachings is Illumination. Illumination does not mean that some new organ or object has been acquired or attached to the physical body. Illumination means that the faculties and potentialities of your body and mind and Soul Unit have been so developed and strengthened by a strenuous Course of Training, that the powers which are innately inherent within you, are functioning in a much greater harmony than ever before; that your harmony is sufficient to enable you to be in complete attunement with the Cosmic Consciousness, and become ONE with it.

Illumination is that state in which man is consciously aware of his Soul; wherein he becomes One with the Light and Wisdom of his Soul, and because of the Oneness of All Souls, he in time, becomes conscious of the Whole.

ESOTERIC SCHOOL OF TRUTH

The Great White Lodge is in truth an actual organized body of living Teachers, having in their charge, the keeping of the Sacred Science. Now they live secluded, owing to the hostile attitude which for many centuries mankind has shown, but once the whole World knew and honored the Way of the Initiates. No man rose so high in the state, in philosophy, science, or generalship, that to be admitted to the knowledge of the Mysteries was not considered as great an honor as any the world could bestow. Now the Mysteries have ceased to be openly celebrated, but the Great Centers from which they originally sprang, still exist, as they have existed from untold ages.

From these Centers, age after age, as the world needed guidance, Leaders have been sent forth. As far back as the record of our race can carry us, we catch glimpses of Great Beings, Law Givers, Philosophers, Sages, Magis, Kings, and Priests, all of whom, if we may trust the general outline of history, were in possession of powers and of knowledge which have since become lost temporarily to all but the few who know.

The Ancient Sages and the Great Souls who consecrated their entire lives, generation after generation, to the investigation of the laws of the Universe, reside in the Orient in the heights of the Himalayas. Working alone in the silence, they transmitted the knowledge which they acquired, to trusted disciples only, who starting from the data supplied by these Great Masters, made many more discoveries and transmitted them in turn; so that today the Body of Initiates is in possession of knowledge which the generality of man would be incapable of suspecting and whose results, if they should be suddenly revealed, would appear to material scientists as miraculous and even as impossible to believe.

In this aspect certainly the Sacred Science deserves the respectful consideration of all men, its transcendental truths come to us with authority derived from their own nature and emphasized by their hoary antiquity. The forces to be investigated are so stupendous that only those who have developed themselves spiritually beyond the thrall of envy, jealousy, hatred, and kindred passions, can control them without widespread devastation. Not to the first comer will the Veil of Isis be at once lifted; many and arduous are the tests, almost insurmountable the obstacles, next to impossible the conditions over which the aspirant is required to triumph, and many years of hard endeavor may be the price which he has to pay for the solution of nature's riddles. But never has an earnest disciple been turned away. "To him who knocks at the door it shall be opened and to him who asketh it shall be given."

For many centuries, few have knocked at these Ancient Portals, for the mind of the world has been on wars, conquest, and the lust of wealth. Men have lived in the indulgence of the desires of the flesh and the defense of the physical being. Now, however, with a new era, is coming about a new order of things, the soul is weary of striving and useless toil, and again men are knocking and asking as of old, for the Light of Truth.

In answer to this growing demand, even though it is at present feeble, Great Masters of Esoterism have sent out once again from their midst, envoys, teachers with powers, to establish Schools and Centers of Instructions in all countries where the cry is heard, so that the hungry may be fed, and the aspiring soul may be brought in touch with the Divine Mysteries. To the true Seeker for Truth, the Message of the Great Ones will bring Life, Light, and Peace.

THE RECOVERY OF THE EMERALD TABLETS

When Dr. Doreal completed his studies with the Great Ones of Tibet, he was given special specific assignments. One of those was retrieving the lost Emerald Tablets of Thoth-the-Atlantean. The Tablets had resided in an ancient Temple of the Sun God in the jungles of Yucatan. Doreal was instructed to recover and return these Tablets to the Great Pyramid in Egypt. He carried out this mission successfully in 1925, and was given permission to translate and retain a copy of the wisdom engraved on the Tablets. He suffered many trials, hardships, and tribulations in retrieving these great Tablets, but the wisdom they contain is a shining Light unto the world.

The Emerald Tablets of Thoth-the-Atlantean, the translation of which you, the reader, now hold within this Volume, is without a doubt the most stupendous collection of the Ancient Wisdom available to mankind. Not only is it the one and only actual Manuscript of Atlantean origin, but within its pages reside one of the most complete compendiums of Ancient Wisdom from any age of time. The fact that their origin supersedes the recorded history of civilization, as modern man knows it, attests to its great value. Now, for all time, mankind has access to the greatest mystical Truths ever preserved.

Doreal, being the Master of Time and Space, has accepted the role of Teacher and Guru to mankind, not only in this present age, but he has lived that role many, many times down through the past history of man. In the days of Atlantis, Doreal was known as Horlet, the Dweller, whose story is told in the Emerald Tablets. Horlet, the Great Teacher of Thoth, receives a prominent place in Thoth's epic autobiographical story of

Spiritual Achievement. Doreal, as Horlet on Atlantis, was the Great Spiritual Teacher, not only of Thoth, but to all the Atlanteans. Horlet was the one who taught Thoth the Hidden Mysteries and guided him into his full Illumination. It seems almost impossible for many of us today to realize the Spiritual Magnitude, Light and Purity of Dr. M. Doreal.

THE TEACHINGS OF THE BROTHERHOOD

The Brotherhood of the White Temple was organized for the sole purpose of spreading the Light of Truth to a world just emerging from darkness into Light.

Our world today is in a condition of chaos, in great part, caused by the struggle of consciousness to emerge from the condition of negation and darkness in which it has been submerged for Ages. Man is struggling for light and truth, but unable to find it in a world of darkness, he turns upon that world, unconsciously, and strives to destroy it. The Great Masters of Wisdom, the Elder Brothers of man, have the mighty purpose and plan of guiding man into the perfect Light of Truth. For the carrying out of this purpose, they have appointed certain Ones to open the Pathway to the Light of Higher Spiritual Truth. One of these, so appointed, is Doreal, who, under the direction of the Elder Brothers, formed the Brotherhood as a channel through which knowledge of the Divine Path of Light could be given to the suffering world.

Each individual, by developing his own Spiritual nature, helps to bring greater Light to a world of darkness.

It is the purpose of the Brotherhood to instruct all Seekers in the way by which they may purify the White Temple of their bodies, so that they may be perfect channels of expression for the pure White Light of the Soul.

"Truth is a jewel of an infinite number of facets, with a new face ever turned toward the Light." With this understanding of Truth, it is easy to see why it is necessary for the student to be instructed by One who has examined all aspects of the Jewel of Truth as related to man.

The Brotherhood teaches that the foundation of all development in the Spiritual is through the mastery of the conditions which manifest here in the material world.

It teaches the three-fold development of body, mind and soul, for it knows that each supplements and completes the other.

The Laws and Principles which give us mastery of body, mind and soul must be understood and used, so that we may make ourselves ready for the Inner Master to appear.

When one masters and balances their inner and outer nature, then they become a channel for the Inner Spiritual Light to manifest through. Each one who becomes so Illumined becomes a channel through which the Light of the Great Spiritual Sun may shine to bring Light into a world of darkness.

Doreal, through the Brotherhood, can show you the Way to find this Inner Light and bring it into manifestation, to Light the world of darkness by one more ray of the Divine Light.

Jesus said, "He who is not for me, is against me." Are you

enlisted on the side of Light or darkness? Do you want to make yourself ready for the Master to appear?

It is your choice; no one may decide for you, for each soul has free will to accept or reject. If you desire to enlist on the side of Light to help bring Peace and Light to a world of chaos and darkness, then it is your right and duty to become one of the Brotherhood, coordinating your efforts with those who are working to manifest the Divine Light. Lift yourself up so that all men struggling in darkness may be drawn to you.

Complete information about the Brotherhood may be secured by asking for FREE Literature from:

BROTHERHOOD OF THE WHITE TEMPLE
7830 OAK WAY
SEDALIA, COLORADO 80135
PHONE 303 688–3998
WEB SITE: www.bwtemple.org

PREFACE

The history of the tablets translated in the following pages is strange and beyond the belief of the modern scientists. Their antiquity is stupendous, dating back some 36,000 years B.C. The writer is Thoth, an Atlantean priest-king, who founded a colony in ancient Egypt after the sinking of the mother country. He was the builder of the Great Pyramid of Gizeh, erroneously attributed to Cheops. (See "Great Pyramid", by Doreal.) In it he incorporated his knowledge of the ancient wisdom, and also securely secreted records and instruments of ancient Atlantis.

For some 16,000 years he ruled the ancient race of Egypt, from approximately 50,000 B.C. to 36,000 B.C. At that time the ancient barbarous race among which he and his followers had settled had been raised to a high degree of civilization. Thoth was an immortal, that is, had conquered death, passing only when he willed, and even then, not through death. His vast wisdom made him ruler over the various Atlantean colonies, including the ones in South and Central America.

When the time came for him to leave Egypt he erected the Great Pyramid over the entrance to the Great Halls of Amenti, placed in it his records and appointed guards for his secrets from among the highest of his people. In later times the descendants of these guards became the Pyramid Priests, while Thoth was deified as the God of Wisdom, the Recorder, by those in the age of darkness which followed his passing. In legend, the Halls of Amenti became the underworld, the Halls of the Gods, where the soul passed after death, for judgment.

During later ages the ego of Thoth passed into the bodies of men in the manner described in the Tablets. As such he incarnated three times, in his last being known as Hermes, the thrice-born. In this incarnation he left the writing known to modern occultists as the Emerald Tablets, a later and far lesser exposition of the ancient mysteries.

The Tablets translated in this work are ten of twelve which were left in the Great Pyramid in the custody of the Pyramid Priests. The ten are divided into thirteen parts for the sake of convenience. The last two are so great and far reaching in their import that at present it is forbidden to release them to the world at large. However, in those contained herein are secrets which will prove of inestimable value to the serious student. They should be read, not once, but a hundred times for only thus can the true meaning be revealed. A casual reading will give glimpses of beauty, but more intensive study will open avenues of wisdom to the seeker.

But now a word as to how these mighty secrets came to be revealed to modern man after being hidden so long.

Some thirteen hundred years B.C., Egypt, the ancient Khem, was in turmoil and many delegations of priests were sent to other parts of the world. Among these were some of the Pyramid Priests who carried with them the Emerald Tablets as a talisman by which they could exercise authority over the less advanced priest-craft of races descended from other Atlantean colonies. The tablets were understood from legend to give the bearer authority from Thoth.

The particular group of priests bearing the Tablets emigrated to South America where they found a flourishing race, the Mayas, who remembered much of the Ancient Wisdom. Among these the priests settled and remained. In the tenth century the Mayas had thoroughly settled Yucatan and the Tablets were placed beneath the altar of one of the great temples of the Sun God. After the conquest of the Mayas by the Spaniards the cities were abandoned and the treasures of the temples forgotten.

It should be understood that the Great Pyramid of Egypt has been, and still is, a temple of initiation into the mysteries. Jesus, Solomon, Appolonius and others were initiated there. The writer who has a connection with the Great White Lodge, which also works through the Pyramid Priest-hood was instructed to recover, and return to the Great Pyramid the Ancient Tablets. This, after adventures which need not be detailed here, was accomplished. Before returning them he was given permission to translate and retain a copy of the wisdom engraved on the Tablets. This was done in 1925 and only now has permission been given for part to be published. It is expected that many will scoff, yet the true student will read between the lines and gain wisdom. If the light is in you, the light which is engraved in these Tablets will respond.

Now, a word as to the material aspect of the Tablets. They consist of twelve tablets of Emerald green, formed from a substance, created through alchemical transmutation. They are imperishable, resistant to all elements and substance. In effect the atomic and cellular structure is fixed, no change ever taking place. In this respect they violate the material law of ionization. Upon them are engraved characters in the ancient Atlantean language; characters which respond to attuned thought waves, releasing the associated mental vibration in the mind of the reader. The Tablets are fastened together with hoops of a golden colored alloy suspended from a rod of the same material. So much for the material appearance. The wisdom contained therein is the foundation of the ancient mysteries, and for the one who reads with open eyes, and mind, his wisdom shall be increased a hundredfold.

Read, believe or not, but read, and the vibration found therein will awaken a response in your soul.

In Cosmic Harmony,
Doreal
Supreme Voice of the Brotherhood

EMERALD TABLETS

TABLET I

THE HISTORY OF THOTH, THE ATLANTEAN

I, THOTH, the Atlantean, master of mysteries, keeper of records, mighty king, magician, living from generation to generation, being about to pass into the Halls of Amenti, set down for the guidance of those that are to come after, these records of the mighty wisdom of Great Atlantis.

In the great city of KEOR, on the island of UNDAL, in a time far past, I began this incarnation; not as the little men of the present age did the mighty ones of Atlantis live and die but rather from aeon to aeon, did they renew their life in the Halls of Amenti, where the river of life flows eternally onward.

A hundred times ten have I descended the dark way that led into light, and as many times have I ascended from the darkness into the light, my strength and power renewed.

Now for a time I descend and the men of KHEM shall know me no more, but in a time yet unborn will I rise again, mighty and potent, requiring an accounting of those left behind me. Then beware, O men of KHEM, if ye have falsely betrayed my teaching for I shall cast ye down from your high estate into the darkness of the caves from whence ye came. Betray not my secrets to the men of the North, or the men of the South, lest my curse fall upon ye. Remember, and heed my words, for surely will I return again and require of thee that which ye guard, aye, even from beyond time and from beyond death will I return, rewarding or punishing as ye have requited your trust.

Great were my people in the ancient days, great beyond the conception of the little people now around me; knowing wisdom of old, seeking far within the heart of infinity, knowledge that belonged to earth's youth. Wise were we with the wisdom of the Children of Light who dwelt amongst us, strong were we with the power drawn from the eternal fire; and of all these, greatest among the children of men was my father, THOTME, keeper of the great temple, link between the Children of Light, who dwelt within the temple and the races of men who inhabited the ten islands. Mouthpiece after the three, of the Dweller of UNAL, speaking to the Kings with the voice that must be obeyed.

Grew I there from a child into manhood, being taught by my father, the elder mysteries, until in time there grew within the fire of wisdom, until it burst into a consuming flame. Naught desired I but the attainment of wisdom, until on a great day the command came from the Dweller of the Temple that I be brought before him. Few there were among the children of men who had looked upon that mighty face and lived, for not as the sons of men, are the Children of Light when they are not incarnate in a physical body.

Chosen was I from the sons of men, taught by the Dweller so that his purposes might be fulfilled, purposes yet unborn in the womb of time. Long ages I dwelt in the Temple, learning ever and yet ever more wisdom, until I too approached the light emitted from the great fire. Taught me he, the path to Amenti, the underworld where the great king sits upon his throne of might. Deep I bowed in homage before the Lords of Life and the Lords of Death, receiving as my gift the Key of Life. Free was I of the Halls of Amenti, bound not by death to the circle of life. Far to the stars I journeyed until space and time became as naught. Then having drunk deep of the cup of wisdom I looked into the hearts of men, and there found I yet greater mysteries and was glad, for only in the Search for Truth could my Soul be stilled, and the flame within be quenched.

Down through the ages I lived, seeing those around me taste of the cup of death and return again in the light of life. Gradually from the Kingdoms of Atlantis passed the waves of consciousness that had been one with me, only to be replaced by spawn of a lower star.

In obedience to the law, the word of the Master grew into flower. Downward into darkness turned the thoughts of the Atlanteans, until at last in his wrath arose from his AGWANTI (here is a word for which we have no English equivalent; it means a state of detachment) the Dweller, speaking the Word, calling the power; deep in earth's heart the sons of Amenti heard, and hearing, directed the changing of the flower of fire that burns eternally, changing and shifting, using the LOGOS, until that great fire changed its direction.

Over the world then, broke the great waters drowning and sinking, changing earth's balance until only the Temple of Light was left standing on the great mountain on UNDAL still rising out of the water; some there were who were living, saved from the rush of the fountains.

Called to me then the Master, saying: "Gather ye together my people, take them by the arts ye have learned of, far across the waters, until ye reach the land of the hairy barbarians, dwelling in caves of the desert; follow there the plan that ye know of."

Gathered I then, my people and entered the great ship of the Master; upward we rose into the morning, dark beneath us lay the Temple, suddenly over it rose the waters, vanished from earth, until the time appointed, was the great Temple. Fast we fled toward the sun of the morning, until beneath us lay the land of the children of KHEM. Raging, they came, with cudgels and spears, lifted in anger, seeking to slay and utterly destroy the Sons of Atlantis. Then raised I my staff and directed a ray of vibration, striking them still in their tracks, as fragments of stone of the mountain. Then spoke I to them in words calm and peaceful, telling them of the might of Atlantis, saying we were children of the Sun and its messengers. Cowed I them by my display of magic-science, until at my feet they groveled, when I released them.

Long dwelt we in the land of KHEM, long and yet long again, until obeying the commands of the Master, who while sleeping, yet lives eternally, I sent from me the Sons of Atlantis; sent them in many directions, that from the womb of time wisdom might rise again in her children.

Long time then dwelt I in the land of KHEM, doing great works by the wisdom within me. Upward grew into the light of knowledge the children of KHEM, watered by the rains of my wisdom. Blasted I then a path to Amenti, so that I might retain my power, living from age to age, a Sun of Atlantis, keeping the wisdom, preserving the records.

Great grew the sons of KHEM, conquering the people around them, growing slowly upwards in Soul force. Now for a time I go from among them, into the dark halls of Amenti, deep in the halls of earth, before the Lords of the powers, face to face once again with the Dweller.

Raised I high over the entrance a doorway, a gateway leading down to Amenti. Few there would be with courage to dare it, few pass the portal to dark Amenti. Raised over the passage, I, a mighty pyramid, using the power that overcomes earth force (gravity). Deep and yet deeper placed I a force-house or chamber; from it carved I a circular passage, reaching almost to the great summit. There in the apex set I the crystal, sending the ray into the "Time-Space", drawing the force from out of the ether, concentrating upon the gateway to Amenti. (See "The Great Pyramid", by Doreal.)

Other chambers I built and left vacant to all seeming, yet hidden within them are the keys to Amenti. He who in courage, would dare the dark realms, let him be purified first by long fasting, lie in the sarcophagus of stone in my chamber, then reveal I to him the great mysteries. Soon shall he follow to where I shall meet him, even in the darkness of earth shall I meet him, I, Thoth, Lord of Wisdom, meet him and hold him, and dwell with him always.

Builded I the Great Pyramid, patterned after the pyramid of earth force, burning eternally, so that it too might remain through the ages. In it I builded my knowledge of "Magic-Science", so that it might be here when again I return from Amenti. Aye, while I sleep in the Halls of Amenti, my Soul roaming free will incarnate, dwell among men in this form or another. (Hermes, thrice-born.)

Emissary on earth am I of the Dweller, fulfilling his commands so man might be lifted. Now return I to the Halls of Amenti, leaving behind me some of my wisdom. Preserve ye and keep ye the command of the Dweller, lift ever upwards your eyes toward the light. Surely in time, ye are one with the Master, surely by right ye are one with the Master, surely by right ye are one with the ALL.

Now, I depart from ye, know my commandments, keep them and be them, and I will be with you, helping and guiding you into the Light.

Now before me opens the portal, go I down in the darkness of night.

EMERALD TABLETS

TABLET II

THE HALLS OF AMENTI

Deep in earth's heart lie the Halls of Amenti, far neath the islands of sunken Atlantis, Halls of the Dead, and halls of the living, bathed in the fire of the infinite All.

Far in a past time, lost in the space time, the Children of Light looked down on the world; seeing th e children of men in their bondage, bound by the force that came from beyond; knew they that only by freedom from bondage could man ever rise from the earth to the Sun. Down they descended and created bodies, taking the semblance of men as their own. The Masters of everything said after their forming, "We are they who were formed from the space-dust, partaking of life from the infinite All; living in the world as children of men, like and yet unlike the children of men."

Then for a dwelling place, far neath the earth crust, blasted great spaces, they by their power, spaces apart from the children of men. Surrounded them by forces and power, shielded from harm, they the Halls of the Dead.

Side by side then, placed they, other spaces, filled them with Life, and with Light from above. Builded they then the Halls of Amenti, that they might dwell eternally there, living with life to eternity's end.

Thirty and two were there of the children, sons of Light who had come among men, seeking to free from the bondage of darkness, those who were bound by the force from beyond.

Deep in the Halls of Life grew a flower, flaming, expanding, driving backward the night. Placed in the center a ray of great potence, Life giving, Light giving, filling with power all who came near it. Placed they around it thrones, two and thirty, places for each of the Children of Light, placed so that they were bathed in the radiance, filled with the Life from the eternal Light. There time after time placed they their first created bodies, so that they might be filled with the Spirit of Life.

One hundred years out of each thousand, must the Life giving Light flame forth on their bodies, quickening, awakening the Spirit of Life.

There in the circle from aeon to aeon, sit the Great Masters, living a life not known among men. There in the Halls of Life they lie sleeping; free flows their Soul through the bodies of men. Time after time, while their bodies lie sleeping, incarnate they in the bodies of men. Teaching and guiding onward and upward, out of the darkness into the light. There in the Hall of Life, filled with their wisdom, known not to the races of man, living forever neath the cold fire of life, sit the Children of Light. Times there are when they awaken, come from the depths to be lights among men, infinite they among finite men.

He who by progress has grown from the darkness, lifted himself from the night into light, free is he made of the Halls of Amenti, free of the flower of Light and of Life. Guided he then, by wisdom and knowledge, passes from men, to the Master of Life. There he may dwell as one with the Masters, free from the bonds of the darkness of night.

Seated within the flower of radiance sit seven Lords from the Space-Times above us, helping and guiding through infinite Wisdom, the pathway through time, of the children of men. Mighty and strange, they, veiled with their power, silent, all knowing, drawing the Life force, different, yet one with the children of men, aye, different and yet one with the Children of Light.

Custodians, and watchers of the force of man's bondage, ready to loose when the light has been reached. First and most mighty, sits the Veiled Presence, Lord of Lords, the infinite Nine, over the others from each Cosmic cycle, weighing and watching the progress of men.

Under HE, sit the Lords of the Cycles; Three, Four, Five, and Six, Seven, Eight, each with his mission, each with his powers, guiding, directing the destiny of man. There sit they, mighty and potent, free of all time and space, not of this world they, yet akin to it, Elder Brothers they, of the children of men. Judging and weighing, they with their wisdom, watching the progress of Light among men.

There before them was I led by the Dweller, watched him blend with ONE from above, then from HE came forth a voice saying, "Great art thou, Thoth, among children of men. Free henceforth of the Halls of Amenti, Master of Life among children of men. Taste not of death except as thou will it, drink thou of Life to Eternity's end. Henceforth forever is Life, thine for the taking, henceforth is Death at the call of thy hand. Dwell here or leave here, when thou desireth, free is Amenti to the Sun of man. Take thou up Life in what form thou desireth, Child of the Light that has grown among men. Choose thou thy work, for all Souls must labor, never be free from the pathway of Light. One step thou hast gained on the long pathway upward, infinite now is the mountain of Light. Each step thou taketh but heightens the mountain, all of thy progress but lengthens the goal, approach ye ever the infinite Wisdom, ever before thee recedes the goal. Free are ye made now of the Halls of Amenti, to walk hand in hand with the Lords of the world, one in one purpose, working together, bringers of Light to the children of men."

Then from his throne came one of the Masters, taking my hand and leading me onward, through all the Halls of the deep hidden land. Led he me through the Halls of Amenti, showing the mysteries that are known not to man. Through the dark passage downward he led me into the Hall where sits the dark Death. Vast as space lay the great Hall before me, walled by darkness, but yet filled with Light.

Before me arose a great throne of darkness, veiled on it seated a figure of night. Darker than darkness sat the great figure, dark with a darkness not of the night. Before it then paused the Master, speaking the Word that brings about Life, saying, "Oh, master of darkness, guide of the way from Life unto Life, before thee I bring a Sun of the morning, touch him not ever with the power of night, call not his flame to the darkness of night. Know him and see him, one of our brothers, lifted from darkness into the Light. Release thou his flame from its bondage, free let it flame through the darkness of night."

Raised then the hand of the figure, forth came a flame that grew clear and bright. Rolled back swiftly the curtain of darkness, unveiled the Hall from the darkness of night. Then grew in the great space before me, flame after flame, from the veil of the night, uncounted millions leaped they before me, some flaming forth as flowers of fire, others there were that shed a dim radiance, glowing but faintly from out of the night. Some there were that faded swiftly, others that grew from a small spark of light. Each surrounded by its dim veil of darkness, yet flaming with light that could never be quenched, coming and going like fireflies in springtime, filled they the space with Light and with Life.

Then spoke a voice, mighty and solemn, saying: "These are lights, that are souls among men, growing and fading, existing forever, changing yet living, through death into life. When they have bloomed into flower, reached the zenith of growth in their life, swiftly then send I my veil of darkness, shrouding and changing to new forms of life. Steadily upward throughout the ages, growing, expanding into yet greater flame, lighting the darkness with yet greater power, quenched yet unquenched by the veil of the night. So grows the Soul of man ever upward, quenched yet unquenched by the darkness of night.

"I, Death, come, and yet I remain not, for life eternal exists in the all; only an obstacle, I in the pathway, quick to be conquered by the infinite light. Awaken, Oh flame that burns ever inward, flame forth and conquer the veil of the night."

Then in the midst of the flames in the darkness grew there one that drove forth the night, flaming, expanding, ever brighter, until at last was nothing but Light. Then spoke my guide, the voice of the master, "See your own Soul as it grows in the light, free now forever from the Lord of the night."

Forward he led me through many great spaces filled with the mysteries of the Children of Light; mysteries that man may never yet know of until he too is a Sun of the Light. Backward then HE led me into the Light of the Hall of the Light, knelt I then before the great Masters, Lords of All from the cycles above.

Spoke HE then with words of great power saying: "Thou hast been made free of the Halls of Amenti, choose thou thy work among the children of men."

Then spoke I: "Oh, great master, let me be a teacher of men, leading them onward and upward, until they too are lights among men. Freed from the veil of the night that surrounds them, flaming with light that shall shine among men."

Spoke to me then the voice; "Go, as ye will, so be it decreed. Master are ye of your destiny, free to take or reject at will. Take ye the power, take ye the wisdom, shine as a light among the children of men."

Upward then, led me the Dweller, dwelt I again among children of men; teaching and showing some of my wisdom, Sun of the Light, a fire among men.

Now again I tread the path downward, seeking the light in the darkness of night. Hold ye and keep ye, preserve my record, guide shall it be to the children of men.

EMERALD TABLETS

TABLET III

THE KEY OF WISDOM

I, Thoth, the Atlantean, give of my wisdom; give of my knowledge; give of my power; freely I give to the children of men. Give, that they too might have wisdom, to shine through the world from the veil of the night. Wisdom is power and power is wisdom, one with each other, perfecting the whole.

Be thou not proud, Oh Man! in thy wisdom; discourse with the ignorant, as well as the wise. If one comes to thee full of knowledge, listen and heed, for wisdom is all.

Keep thou not silent when evil is spoken, for Truth, like the sunlight, shines above all.

He who over-steppeth the Law shall be punished, for only through Law comes the freedom of men.

Cause thou not fear for fear is a bondage, a fetter that binds the darkness to men.

Follow thine heart during thy lifetime; do thou more than is commanded of thee.

When thou has't gained riches, follow thou thine heart, for all these are of no avail if thine heart be weary. Diminish thou not the time of following thine heart, it is abhorred of the Soul.

They that are guided go not astray, but they that are

lost cannot find a straight path. If thou go among men, make for thyself, Love, the beginning and end of the heart.

If one cometh unto thee for council, let him speak freely, that the thing for which he hath come to thee may be done. If he hesitates to open his heart to thee, it is because thou, the judge, doeth the wrong.

Repeat thou not extravagant speech, neither listen thou to it, for it is the utterance of one not in equilibrium. Speak thou not of it, so that he, before thee may know wisdom.

Silence is of great profit, an abundance of speech profiteth nothing.

Exalt not thine heart above the children of men, lest it be brought lower than the dust.

If thou be great among men, be honoured for knowledge and gentleness.

If thou seeketh to know the nature of a friend, ask not his companion, but pass a time alone with him. Debate with him, testing his heart by his words and his bearing.

That which goeth into the store-house must come forth and the things that are thine must be shared with a friend.

Knowledge is regarded by the fool as ignorance, and the things that are profitable are to him hurtful; he liveth in death, it is therefore his food.

The wise man lets his heart overflow, but keeps silent his mouth.

Oh men! list to the voice of wisdom; list to the voice of light. Mysteries there are in the Cosmos, that unveiled fill the world with their light. Let he who would be free from the bonds of darkness first divine the material from the immaterial, the fire from the earth; for know ye that as earth descends to earth, so also fire ascends unto fire and becomes one with fire. He who knows the fire that is within himself shall ascend unto the eternal fire and dwell in it eternally.

Fire, the inner fire, is the most potent of all force, for it overcometh all things, and penetrates to all things of the earth.

Man supports himself only on that which resists, so earth must resist man else he existeth not.

All eyes do not see with the same vision, for to one an object appears of one form and color and to a different eye of another, so also the infinite fire, changing from color to color is never the same from day to day.

Thus, speak I, THOTH, of my wisdom for man is a fire burning bright through the night, never is quenched in the veil of the darkness, never is quenched by the veil of the night.

Into men's hearts, I looked by my wisdom, found them not free from the bondage of strife. Free from the toils, thy fire, oh my brother! lest it be buried in the shadow of night.

Hark ye, oh man! and list to this wisdom, where do name and form cease? Only in consciousness, invisible, an infinite force of radiance bright. The forms that ye create by brightening thy vision, are truly effects that follow thy cause.

Man is a star bound to a body until in the end he is freed through his strife. Only by struggle and toiling thy utmost shall the star within thee bloom out in new life. He who knows the commencement of all things, free is his star from the realms of night.

Remember, Oh man! that all which exists is only another form of that which exists not. Everything that has being is passing into yet other being, and thou thyself are not an exception.

Consider the Law, for all is Law, seek not that which is not of the Law, for such exists only in the illusions of the senses.

Wisdom cometh to all her children, even as they cometh unto wisdom.

All through the ages the light has been hidden; awake, Oh man! and be wise.

Deep in the mysteries of life have I traveled, seeking and searching for that which is hidden. List Ye, Oh man! and be wise.

Far neath the earth crust, in the Halls of Amenti, mysteries I saw, that are hidden from men.

Oft have I journeyed the deep hidden passage, looked on the Light, that is Life among men. There neath the flowers of Life ever living, searched I the hearts, and the secrets of men. Found I that man is but living in darkness, light of the great fire is hidden within.

Before the Lords of hidden Amenti learned I the wisdom I give unto men. Masters are they of the great Secret Wisdom, brought from the future of infinity's end. Seven are they, the Lords of Amenti, overlords they of the Children of Morning, Suns of the cycles, Masters of Wisdom, formed are not they as the children of men. Three, Four, Five and Six, Seven, Eight—Nine are the titles of the Masters of men.

Far from the future, formless, yet forming, came they as teachers for the children of men. Live they forever, yet not of the living, bound not to life, and yet free from death. Rule they forever with infinite wisdom, bound, yet not bound to the dark Halls of Death. Life they have in them, yet life that is not life, free from all are the Lords of the All.

Forth from them came forth the Logos, instruments they of the power o'er all. Vast is their countenance, yet hidden in smallness, formed by a forming, known yet unknown.

Three; holds the key of all hidden magic, creator he, of the Halls of the Dead; sending forth power, shrouding with darkness, binding the Souls of the children of men; sending the darkness, binding the Soul force; director of negative, to the children of men.

Four; is he who looses the power, Lord he, of Life, to the children of men. Light is his body, flame is his countenance, freer of Souls to the children of men.

Five; is the master, the Lord of all magic—Key to the WORD that resounds among men.

Six; is the Lord of Light, the hidden pathway, path of the Souls of the children of men.

Seven; is he who is Lord of the vastness, master of Space, and the key of the Times.

Eight; is he who orders the progress, weighs and balances the journey of men.

Nine; is the Father, vast he of countenance, forming and changing from out of the formless.

Meditate on the symbols I give thee, keys are they, though hidden from men.

Reach ever upward O Soul of the morning, turn thy thoughts upward, to light and to Life. Find in the keys of the numbers I bring thee, light on the pathway from life unto life.

Seek ye with wisdom, turn thy thoughts inward, close not thy mind to the flower of Light.

Place in thy body a thought formed picture; think of the numbers that lead thee to Life.

Clear is the pathway to he who has wisdom, open the door to the Kingdom of Light.

Pour forth thy flame as a Sun of the morning, shut out the darkness and live in the day.

Take thee, Oh man! as part of thy being, the seven, who are, but are not as they seem. Opened, Oh man! have I my wisdom, follow the path in the way I have led.

Masters of Wisdom, SUN of the MORNING, LIGHT and LIFE to the children of men.

EMERALD TABLETS

TABLET IV

THE SPACE BORN

List ye, O man, to the voice of wisdom, list to the voice of THOTH, the Atlantean. Freely I give to thee of my wisdom, gathered from the time and space of this cycle; master of mysteries, SUN of the morning, living forever, a child of the LIGHT, shining with brightness, star of the morning, THOTH, the teacher of men, is of all.

Long time ago I, in my childhood, lay neath the stars on long buried ATLANTIS, dreaming of mysteries far above men. Then in my heart, grew there a great longing to conquer the pathway that led to the stars. Year after year I sought after wisdom, seeking new knowledge, following the way, until at last my SOUL, in great travail, broke from its bondage and bounded away. Free was I, from the bondage of earth-man, free from the body, I flashed through the night. Unlocked at last for me was the star-space; free was I from the bondage of night. Now to the end of space sought I wisdom, far beyond knowledge of finite man.

Far into space my SOUL traveled freely, into infinity's circle of light. Strange, beyond knowledge, were some of the planets, great and gigantic, beyond dreams of men. Yet found I law, in all of its beauty, working through and among them, as here among men. Flashed forth my Soul through infinity's beauty, far through space I flew with my thoughts.

Rested I there on a planet of beauty, strains of harmony filled all the air; shapes there were, moving in order, great and majestic as   stars in the night; mounting in harmony, ordered equilibrium, symbols of the Cosmic, like unto law.

Many the stars I passed in my journey, many the races of men on their worlds; some reaching high as stars of the morning, some falling low in the blackness of night. Each and all of them struggling upward, gaining the heights and plumbing the depths, moving at times in realms of brightness, living through darkness, gaining the Light.

Know, O man, that light is thine heritage, know that darkness is only a veil, Sealed in thine heart is brightness eternal, waiting the moment of freedom to conquer, waiting to rend the veil of the night.

Some I found who had conquered the ether, free of space were they, while yet they were men. Using the force that is the foundation of ALL things; far in space constructed they, a planet, drawn by the force that flows through the ALL; condensing, coalescing the ether, into forms that grew as they willed. Outstripping in science they, all of the races, mighty in wisdom, sons of the stars.

Long time I paused, watching their wisdom, saw them create from out of the ether, cities gigantic, of rose and of gold. Formed forth from the primal element, base of all matter, the ether far flung.

Far in the past they had conquered the ether, freed themselves from the bondage of toil; formed in their mind only a picture, and swiftly created it grew.

Forth, then, my Soul sped, throughout the Cosmos, seeing ever, new things and old, learning that man is truly space-born, a Sun of the Sun, a child of the stars.

Know ye, O man, whatever form ye inhabit, surely it is one with the stars. Thy bodies are nothing but planets, revolving around their central suns. When ye have gained the light of all wisdom, free shall   ye be to shine in the ether—one of the Suns that light outer darkness—one of the space-born grown into light. Just as the stars in time lose their brilliance, light passing from them into the great source; so, O man, thy soul passes onward, leaving behind the darkness of night.

Formed forth ye, from the primal ether, filled with the brilliance that flows from the source, bound by the ether coalesced around, yet ever it flames until at last it is free. Lift up your flame from out of the darkness, fly from the night and ye shall be free.

Traveled I through the space-time, knowing my Soul at last was set free; knowing that now might I pursue wisdom, until at last I passed to a plane, hidden from knowledge, known not to wisdom, extension beyond all that we know. Now, O man, when I had this knowing, happy my Soul grew, for now I was free. Listen ye space-born, list to my wisdom, know ye not that ye too will be free.

List ye again, O man, to my wisdom, that hearing, ye too might live and be free, Not of the earth are ye—

earthy, but child of the Infinite Cosmic Light.

Know ye not, O man, of your heritage, know ye not ye are truly the Light? Sun of the Great Sun, when ye gain wisdom, truly aware of your kinship with Light.

Now, to ye, I give knowledge, freedom to walk in the path I have trod, showing ye truly how, by my striving, I trod the path, that leads to the stars.

Hark ye, O man, and know of thy bondage, know how to free thyself from the toils. Out of the darkness shall ye rise upward, one with the light, and one with the stars. Follow ye ever the path of wisdom, only by this can ye rise from below. Ever man's destiny leads him onward, into the Curves of Infinity's All.

Know ye, O man, that all space is ordered, only by order are ye One with the All. Order and balance are the law of the Cosmos, follow and ye shall be One with the All.

He who would follow the pathway of wisdom, open must be, to the flower of life, extending his consciousness out of the darkness, flowing through time and space in the All.

Deep in the silence, first ye must linger, until at last ye are free from desire, free from the longing to speak in the silence, conquer by silence, the bondage of words. Abstaining from eating, until we have conquered desire for food, that is bondage of Soul.

Then lie ye down in the darkness, close ye your eyes from the rays of the light. Center thy Soul-force in the place of thine consciousness, shaking it free from the bonds of the night. Place in thy mind-place the image thou desireth, picture the place thou desireth to see, vibrate back and forth with thy power, loosen the Soul from out of its night. Fiercely must thou shake, with all of thy power, until at last thy Soul shall be free.

Mighty beyond words is the flame of the Cosmic, hanging in planes, unknown to man, mighty and balanced, moving in order, music of harmonies, far beyond man. Speaking with music, singing with color, flame from the beginning of Eternity's All.

Spark of the flame art thou, O my children, burning with color, and living with music; list to the voice and thou shalt be free.

Consciousness free, is fused with the Cosmic, One with the order and law of the All.

Know ye not man, that out of the darkness; light shall flame forth, a symbol of All.

Pray ye this prayer for attaining of wisdom; pray for the coming of light to the All.

"Mighty SPIRIT of LIGHT, that shines through the Cosmos, draw my flame closer in harmony to thee—lift up my fire from out of the darkness, magnet of fire that is One with the All."

"Lift up my Soul, thou mighty and potent, child of the Light, turn not away, draw me in power to melt in thy furnace; One with all things and all things in One, fire of the life-strain and One with the Brain."

When ye have freed thy Soul from its bondage, know that for ye, the darkness is gone. Ever through space ye may seek wisdom, bound not by fetters, forged in the flesh.

Onward and upward into the morning, free flash, O Soul, to the realms of Light. Move thou in order, move thou in harmony, freely shalt move with the Children of Light.

Seek ye and know ye, my KEY of Wisdom, thus, O man, ye shall surely be free.

EMERALD TABLETS

TABLET V

THE DWELLER OF UNAL

Oft dream I of buried Atlantis, lost in the ages that have passed into night. Aeon on aeon thou existed in beauty, a light shining bright through the darkness of night.

Mighty in power, ruling the earth-born, Lord of the earth in Atlantis' day. King of the nations, master of wisdom, LIGHT through SUNTAL, Keeper of the way, dwelt in his TEMPLE, the MASTER of UNAL, LIGHT of the earth in Atlantis' day.

Master, HE, from a cycle beyond us, living in bodies as one among men. Not as the earth-born HE from beyond us, SUN of a cycle, advanced beyond men.

Know ye, O man, that HORLET, the Master, was never one, with the children of men. Far in the past time, when Atlantis first grew as a power, appeared there one with the KEY of WISDOM, showing the way of LIGHT to all.

Showed he, to all men, the path of attainment, way of the Light that flows among men. Mastering darkness, leading the MAN-SOUL, upward to heights that were One with the Light.

Divided the Kingdoms, HE into sections, ten were

they, ruled by children of men. Upon another, built HE a TEMPLE, built, but not by the children of men.

Out of the ETHER called HE its substance, moulded and formed, by the power of YTOLAN, into the forms HE built with His mind. Mile upon mile it covered the island, space upon space it grew in its might. Black, yet not black, but dark like the space-time, deep in its heart the ESSENCE of LIGHT. Swiftly the TEMPLE grew into being, moulded and shaped by the WORD of the DWELLER, called from the formless into a form.

Builded HE then, within it great chambers, filled them with forms called forth from the ETHER, filled them with wisdom called forth by His mind.

Formless was HE within his TEMPLE, yet was HE formed in the image of men. Dwelling among them, yet not of them, strange and far different was HE from the children of men.

Chose HE then, from among the people, THREE who became his gateway, chose HE the THREE from the Highest, to become his links with Atlantis. Messengers they, who carried his council, to the kings of the children of men.

Brought HE forth others and taught them wisdom, teachers they, to the children of men. Place HE them on the island of UNDAL, to stand as teachers of LIGHT to men.

Each of those who were thus chosen, taught must he be for years five and ten, only thus could he have understanding to bring LIGHT to the children of men. Thus there came into being the Temple, a dwelling place for the Master of men.

I, THOTH, have ever sought wisdom, searching in darkness, and searching in Light. Long in my youth I traveled the pathway, seeking ever new knowledge to gain, until after much striving, one of the THREE, to me brought the LIGHT. Brought HE to me the commands of the Dweller, called me from darkness into the LIGHT. Brought HE me, before the DWELLER, deep in the Temple before the great FIRE.

There on the great throne, beheld I, the DWELLER, clothed with the LIGHT and flashing with fire. Down I knelt before that great wisdom, feeling the LIGHT flowing through me in waves. Heard I then the voice of the DWELLER, "O darkness, come into the Light. Long have ye sought the pathway to LIGHT. Each soul on earth that loosens its fetters, shall soon be made free from the bondage of night. Forth from the darkness have ye arisen, closer approached the Light of your goal. Here, ye shall dwell as one of my children, keeper of records gathered by wisdom, instrument thou of the LIGHT from beyond. Ready be thou made, to do what is needed, preserver of wisdom through the ages of darkness, that shall come fast on the children of men. Live thee here and drink of all wisdom, secrets and mysteries unto thee shall unveil."

Then answered I, the MASTER of CYCLES, saying: "O Light, that descended to men; give thou, to me of thy wisdom, that I might be a teacher of men; give thou of thy

LIGHT that I may be free."

Spoke then to me again, the MASTER, "Age after age shall ye live through your wisdom, aye, when o'er Atlantis the ocean waves roll; holding the Light, though hidden in darkness, ready to come when e'er thou shalt call. Go thee now and learn greater wisdom, grow thou, through LIGHT to Infinity's ALL."

Long then dwelt I, in the Temple of the DWELLER, until at last I was One with the LIGHT.

Followed, I then, the path to the star planes; followed I, then, the pathway to LIGHT. Deep into earth's heart I followed the pathway, learning the secrets, below as above; learning the pathway to the HALLS of AMENTI; learning the LAW that balances the world. To earth's hidden chambers pierced I, by my wisdom, deep through the earth's crust, into the pathway, hidden for ages from the children of men. Unveiled before me, ever more wisdom until I reached a new knowledge, found that all is part of an all, great and yet greater than all that we know. Searched I Infinity's heart through the ages, deep and yet deeper, more mysteries I found.

Now, as I look back through the ages, know I that wisdom is boundless, ever grown greater throughout the ages, One with Infinity's greater than all.

Light there was, in ancient ATLANTIS, yet, darkness too was hidden in all. Fell from the Light into the darkness, some who had risen to heights among men. Proud they became, because of their knowledge, proud were they, of their place among men. Deep delved they into the forbidden, opened the gateway that led to below; sought they to gain ever more knowledge, but seeking to bring it up from below.

He who descends below must have balance, else he is bound by lack of our Light. Opened they then, by their knowledge, pathways forbidden to man.

But, in His Temple, all seeing, the DWELLER, lay in his AGWANTI, while through Atlantis His Soul roamed free; saw HE the Atlanteans, by their magic, opening the gateway that would bring to earth, a great woe. Fast fled His Soul, then, back to His body, up HE arose, from His AGWANTI: called HE the Three mighty messengers, gave the commands that shattered the world.

Deep neath earth's crust, to the HALLS of AMENTI, swiftly descended the DWELLER: called HE then, on the powers the Seven Lords wielded, changed the earth's balance; down sank Atlantis, beneath the dark waves.

Shattered the gateway that had been opened, shattered the doorway that led down below. All of the islands were shattered except UNAL, and part of the island of the sons of the DWELLER. Preserved HE them, to be the teachers, lights on the path for those to come after, lights for the lesser children of men.

Called HE them, I, THOTH, before him, gave me commands for all I should do, saying: "Take thou, O THOTH, all of your wisdom, take all your records, take all your magic, go thou forth as a teacher of men; go thou forth, preserving the records until in time, LIGHT grows among men. LIGHT shalt thou be all through the ages, hidden, yet found, by enlightened men. Over all earth, give WE, ye power, free thou to give or to take it away. Gather thou now the sons of Atlantis, take them and flee to the people of the rock caves, fly to the land of the Children of KHEM."

Then gathered I, the sons of Atlantis; into the spaceship I brought all my records, brought the records of sunken Atlantis; gathered I all of my powers, instruments many, of mighty magic.

Up then we rose on wings of the morning, high we arose above the Temple, leaving behind the Three and DWELLER, deep in the HALLS neath the Temple. Down neath the waves sank the great Temple, closing the pathway to the LORDS of the Cycles; yet ever to him, who has knowing, open shall be the path to AMENTI.

Fast fled we then, on the wings of the morning, fled to the land of the children of KHEM. There by my power I conquered and ruled them, raised I to LIGHT, the Children of KHEM.

Deep neath the rocks, I buried my space-ship, waiting the time when man might be free. Over the space-ship, erected a marker in the form of a lion, yet like unto man; there neath the image rests, yet, my space-ship, forth to be brought when need shall arise.

Know ye, O man, that far in the future, invaders shall come from out of the deep; then awake, ye who have wisdom, bring forth my ship and conquer with ease.

Deep neath the image lies my secret, search and find in the pyramid I built. Each to the other, is the Keystone;

each the gateway, that leads into LIFE. Follow the KEY I leave behind me, seek and the doorway to LIFE shall be thine. Seek thou in my pyramid, deep in the passage that ends in a wall, use thou the KEY of the SEVEN, and open to thee, the pathway will fall.

Now, unto thee I have given my wisdom, now unto thee, I have given my way; follow the pathway, solve thou my secrets, unto thee I have shown the way.

TABLET VI

THE KEY OF MAGIC

Hark ye, O man, to the wisdom of magic; hark to the knowledge of powers forgotten. Long, long ago in the days of the first man, warfare began between darkness and light. Men, then, as now, were filled with both darkness and light, and while in some darkness held sway, in others light filled the Soul.

Aye, age old is this warfare, the eternal struggle between darkness and light. Fiercely is it fought all through the ages, using strange powers hidden to man.

Adepts have there been, filled with the blackness, struggling always against the light; but others there are who filled with brightness, have ever conquered the darkness of night. Where e'er ye may be, in all ages and planes, surely ye shall know of the battle with night. Long ages ago the SUNS of the Morning, descending, found the world filled with night. There in that past time began the struggle, the age old battle of darkness and Light.

Many in that time were so filled with darkness, that only feebly flamed the light from the night.

Some there were, masters of darkness who sought to fill all with their darkness; sought to draw others into their night. Fiercely withstood they, the masters of brightness, fiercely fought they, from the darkness of night. Sought they ever to tighten the fetters, the chains that bind man to the darkness of night. Used they always the dark magic, brought into man by the power of darkness, magic that enshrouded man's Soul with darkness.

Banded together in an order, BROTHERS OF DARKNESS, they through the ages, antagonists they, to the children of men. Walked they always, secret and hidden, found, yet not found, by the children of men. Forever, they walked and worked in darkness, hiding from light in the darkness of night. Silently, secretly, use they their power, enslaving and binding the Souls of men.

Unseen they come, and unseen they go, man in his ignorance calls THEM from below.

Dark is the way the DARK BROTHERS travel, dark with a darkness not of the night, traveling o'er earth they walk through man's dreams. Power have they gained from the darkness around them, to call other dwellers from out of their plane. Power have they to direct and send them, in ways that are dark and unseen by man. Into man's mind-space reach the DARK BROTHERS, around it they close the veil of their night. There through its lifetime that Soul dwells in bondage, bound by the fetters, of the VEIL of the night. Mighty are they in the forbidden knowledge, forbidden because it is one with the night.

Hark ye, O man, and list to my warning, be ye free from the bondage of night. Surrender not your Soul to the BROTHERS of DARKNESS, keep thy face ever turned toward the LIGHT. Know ye not, O man, that your sorrow, only, has come through the Veil of the night. Aye, man, heed ye my warning, strive ever upward, turn your Soul toward the LIGHT. The BROTHERS of DARK-

NESS seek for their brothers, those who have traveled the pathway of LIGHT. For well know they, that those who have traveled far towards the SUN on their pathway to LIGHT, have great and yet greater power to bind with darkness the children of LIGHT.

List ye, O man, to he who comes to you, but weigh in the balance, if his words be of LIGHT, for many there are who walk in DARK BRIGHTNESS and yet are not, the Children of LIGHT.

Easy it is to follow their pathway, easy to follow the path that they lead, but yet O man, heed ye my warning, Light comes only to him who strives. Hard is the pathway that leads to the WISDOM, hard is the pathway that leads to the LIGHT. Many shall ye find, the stones in your pathway, many the mountains to climb toward the LIGHT. Yet know ye, O man, to him that o'ercometh, free will he be of the pathway of Light. Follow ye not, the DARK BROTHERS ever, always be ye, a child of the LIGHT. For know ye, O man, in the end LIGHT must conquer, and darkness and night be banished from Light.

Listen, O man, and heed ye this wisdom, even as darkness, so is the LIGHT. When darkness is banished, and all Veils are rended, out there shall flash from the darkness, the LIGHT.

Even as exist among men the DARK BROTHERS, so there exists the BROTHERS of LIGHT. Antagonists they, of the BROTHERS of DARKNESS, seeking to free men from the night. Powers have they, mighty and potent, knowing the LAW, the planets obey. Work they ever in harmony and order, freeing the man-Soul from its bondage of night. Secret and hidden, walk they also, known not are they, to the children of men. Yet know that ever they walk with thee, showing the WAY to the children of men. Ever have THEY fought the DARK BROTHERS, conquered and conquering, time without end. Yet always LIGHT shall in the end be master, driving away the darkness of night.

Aye, man, know ye this knowing, always beside thee, walk the Children of LIGHT.

Masters they of the SUN power, ever unseen, yet the guardians of men. Open to all is their pathway, open to he who will walk in the LIGHT. Free are THEY of DARK AMENTI, free of the HALLS, where LIFE reigns supreme. SUNS are they and LORDS of the morning, Children of Light to shine among men. Like man are they, and yet are unlike, never divided were they in the past. ONE, have they been, in ONENESS eternal, throughout all space since the beginning of time. Up did they come in Oneness with the ALL ONE, up from the first-space, formed and unformed.

Given to man, have they, secrets, that shall guard and protect him from all harm. He who would travel the path of a master, free must he be from the bondage of night. Conquer must he the formless and shapeless, conquer must he the phantom of fear. Knowing, must he gain of all of the secrets, travel the pathway that leads through the darkness, yet ever before him keep the Light of his goal. Obstacles great, shall he meet in the pathway, yet press on to the LIGHT of the SUN.

Hear ye, O man, the SUN is the symbol of the LIGHT that shines at the end of thy road.

Now to thee give I the secrets, how to meet the dark power, meet and conquer the fear from the night. Only by knowing can ye conquer, only by knowing can ye have LIGHT.

Now I give unto thee the knowledge, known to the MASTERS, the knowing that conquers all the dark fears. Use this, the wisdom I give thee, MASTER thou shalt be of the BROTHERS of NIGHT.

When unto thee there comes a feeling, drawing thee nearer to the dark gate, examine thine heart and find if the feeling thou hast, has come from within. If thou shalt find the darkness thine own thoughts, banish them forth from place in thy mind. Send through thy body a wave of vibration, irregular first and regular second, repeating time after time until free. Start the WAVE FORCE in thy BRAIN CENTER, direct it in waves from thine head to thy foot.

But if thou findest thine heart is not darkened, be sure that a force is directed to thee. Only by knowing can thou overcome it, only by wisdom can thou hope to be free. Knowledge brings wisdom and wisdom is power, attain and ye shall have power o'er all.

Seek ye first, a place bound with darkness, place ye a circle around about thee, stand erect in the midst of the circle, use thou this formula and thou shalt be free. Raise thou thine hands to the dark space above thee, close thou thine eyes and draw in the LIGHT. Call to the SPIRIT of LIGHT through the Space-Time, using these words and thou shalt be free: "Fill thou my body, O SPIRIT OF LIFE, fill thou my body with SPIRIT of LIGHT, come from the FLOWER that shines through the darkness, come from the HALLS where the Seven Lords rule. Name them by name, I, the Seven, Three, Four, Five and Six, Seven, Eight—Nine. By their names I call them to aid me, free me and save me from the darkness of night, UNTANAS, QUERTAS, CHIETAL, and GOYANA, HUERTAL, SEMVETA,—ARDAL; by their names I implore thee, free me from darkness and fill me with LIGHT."

Know ye, O man, that when ye have done this, ye shall be free from the fetters that bind ye, cast off the bondage of the BROTHERS of NIGHT. See ye not that the names have the power, to free by vibration the fetters that bind? Use them at need to free thou thine brother, so that he too may come forth from the night.

Thou, O man, art thy brother's helper; let him not lie in the bondage of night.

Now unto thee, give I my magic, take it and dwell on the pathway of LIGHT.

LIGHT unto thee, LIFE unto thee, SUN may thou be on the cycle above.

EMERALD TABLETS

TABLET VII

THE SEVEN LORDS

Hark ye, O man, and list to my Voice, open thy mind-space and drink of my wisdom. Dark is the pathway of LIFE that ye travel, many the pitfalls that lie in thy way. Seek ye, ever, to gain greater wisdom, attain and it shall be light on thy way.

Open thy SOUL, O man, to the Cosmic, and let it flow in as one with thy SOUL. LIGHT is eternal, and darkness is fleeting, seek ye ever, O man, for the LIGHT. Know ye, that ever as light fills thy being, darkness for thee shall soon disappear.

Open thy Soul to the BROTHERS of BRIGHTNESS, let them enter and fill thee with LIGHT. Lift up thine eyes to the LIGHT of the Cosmos, keep thou ever thy face to the goal. Only by gaining the light of all wisdom, art thou one with the Infinite goal. Seek ye ever, the Oneness eternal, seek ye ever the Light of the goal.

Light is infinite, and Light is finite, separate only by darkness in man. Seek ye to rend the Veil of the Darkness, bring thou together the Light into One.

Hear ye, O man, list to my Voice, singing the song of Light and of Life. Throughout all space, Light is prevalent, encompassing ALL, with its banners of flame. Seek ye, forever in the Veil of the Darkness, somewhere ye shall surely find Light. Hidden and buried, lost to man's knowledge, deep in the finite, the Infinite exists. Lost, but existing, flowing through all things, living in ALL is the INFINITE BRAIN.

In all space there is only ONE wisdom, though seeming divided, it is ONE in the ONE. All that exists comes forth from the LIGHT, and the LIGHT comes forth from the All.

Everything created is based upon ORDER: LAW rules the space where the INFINITE dwells. Forth from equilibrium, came the great cycles, moving in harmony toward Infinity's end.

Know ye, O man, that far in the space-time, INFINITY itself shall pass into change. Hear ye, and list to the Voice of Wisdom, know that ALL is of ALL evermore. Know that through time thou may pursue wisdom, and find ever, more light on the way. Aye, thou shalt find that ever receding, thy goal shall elude thee from day unto day.

Long time ago, in the HALLS of AMENTI, I Thoth, stood before the LORDS of the cycles. Mighty, THEY in their aspects of power, mighty THEY, in the wisdom unveiled.

Led by the Dweller, first did I see them, but afterwards free was I of their presence, free to enter their conclave at will. Oft did I journey down the dark pathway unto the HALL where the LIGHT ever glows.

Learned I, of the Masters of cycles, wisdom brought from the cycles above us, knowledge brought from

INFINITY'S ALL. Many the questions I asked, of the LORDS of the cycles, great was the wisdom they gave unto me. Now unto thee I give of this wisdom, drawn from the flame of Infinity's fire.

Deep in the DARK HALLS, sit the Seven, units of consciousness from cycles above, manifest THEY in this cycle, as guides of man to the knowledge of All. Seven are They, mighty in power, speaking these words through me, to men. Time after time, stood I before them listening to words that came not with sound.

Once said THEY unto me, "O man, woulds't thou gain wisdom? Seek for it in the heart of the flame. Woulds't thou gain knowledge of power? Seek ye it in the heart of the flame. Woulds't be One with the heart of the flame? Seek then within thine own hidden flame."

Many the times spoke THEY to me, teaching me wisdom not of the world; showing me, ever, new paths to brightness; teaching me wisdom brought from above. Giving knowledge of operation, learning of LAW, the order of ALL.

Spoke to me again, the Seven, saying: "From far beyond time are WE come, O man, traveled WE, from beyond the SPACE-TIME, aye, from the place of Infinity's end. When ye and all of thy brethren were formless, formed forth were WE from the order of ALL. Not as men, are WE, though once WE too were as men. Out of the Great Void were WE formed forth, in order and by LAW. For know ye, that that which is formed, truly is formless, having form only to thine eyes."

And again unto me spoke the Seven, saying: "Child of the LIGHT, O THOTH, art thou, free to travel the bright path upward, until at the last ALL ONES become ONE.

"Forth were WE formed after our order, Three, Four, Five and Six, Seven, Eight—Nine, Know ye, that these are the number of the cycles that WE descend from, unto man. Each having, here a duty to fulfill, each having here a force to control. Yet are we ONE, with the SOUL of our cycle, yet are WE too, seeking a goal. Far beyond man's conception, Infinity extends into a greater than all. There in a time that is yet not a time, we shall ALL become One, with a greater than ALL. Time and space are moving in circles, know ye their law and ye too shall be free; aye, free shall ye be to move through the cycles—pass the guardians that dwell at the door."

Then to me spoke HE of NINE, saying: "Aeons and aeons have I existed, knowing not LIFE and tasting not death. For know ye, O man, that far in the future, Life and death shall be One with the ALL. Each so perfected by balancing the other, that neither exists in the Oneness of all. In men of this cycle the Life force is rampant, but life in its growth becomes one with the All. Here, I manifest in this, your cycle, but yet am I there in your future of time, yet to me time exists not, for in my world time exists not, for formless are WE. Life have WE not, but yet have existence, fuller and greater and freer than thee.

"Man is a flame bound to a mountain, but WE in our cycle shall ever be free. Know ye, O man, that when ye have progressed into the cycles that lengthen above, life itself will pass to the darkness, and only the essence of Soul shall remain."

Then to me spoke, the LORD of the EIGHT, saying: "All that ye know is but part of little, not as yet have ye touched on the Great. Far out in space where LIGHT reigns supreme, came I into the LIGHT, formed was I also but not as ye are.

"Body of Light, was my formless form, formed; know I not LIFE, and know I not DEATH, yet master am I of all that exists. Seek ye, to find the path through the barriers, travel the road that lead to the LIGHT."

Spoke again to me the NINE, saying: "Seek ye to find the path to beyond; not impossible is it to grow to a consciousness above, for when TWO have become ONE and ONE has become the ALL, know ye the barrier has lifted and ye are made free of the road, Grow thou from form to the formless, free may thou be of the road."

Thus through ages I listened, learning the way to the All. Now lift I my thought to the ALL-THING, list ye, and hear when it calls.

"O LIGHT, all pervading, One with All, and All with One, flow thou to me through the channel, enter thou so that I may be free. Make me One with the ALL-SOUL, shining from the blackness of night. Free, let me be of all space-time, free from the Veil of the night. I, a child of the LIGHT command, free from the darkness to be."

Formless am I to the Light-Soul, formless yet shining

with light. Know I, the bonds of the darkness, must shatter and fall before light. Now give I this wisdom, free may ye be, O man, living in light and in brightness, turn not thy face from the Light, thy Soul dwells in realms of brightness, ye are a child of the Light.

Turn thy thoughts inward, not outward, find thou the Light-Soul within, know that thou art the MASTER, all else is brought from within. Grow thou to realms of brightness, hold thou thy thought on the light, know thou art one with the Cosmos, a flame and a Child of the Light.

Now to thee give I warning, let not thy thoughts turn away, know that the brightness flows through thy body for aye. Turn not to the DARK-BRIGHTNESS that comes from the BROTHERS of BLACK, but keep thine eyes ever lifted, thy Soul in tune with the Light.

Take ye this wisdom and heed it, list to my Voice and obey, follow the pathway to brightness, and thou shalt be ONE with the way.

EMERALD TABLETS

TABLET VIII

THE KEY OF MYSTERIES

Unto thee, O man, have I given my knowledge, unto thee have I given of Light. Hear ye, now, and receive my wisdom, brought from space planes, above and beyond.

Not as man, am I, for free have I become of dimensions and planes. In each take I on a new body, in each I change in my form. Know I now that the formless, is all there is of form.

Great is the wisdom of the Seven, mighty are THEY from beyond, manifest THEY through their power, filled by force from beyond.

Hear ye, these words of wisdom, hear ye, and make them thine own, find in them the formless, find ye the key to beyond. Mystery is but hidden knowledge, know and ye shall unveil, find the deep buried wisdom, and be master of darkness and light.

Deep are the mysteries around thee, hidden the secrets of Old, search through the KEYS of my WISDOM, surely shall ye find the way. The gateway to power is secret, but he who attains shall receive. Look to the LIGHT! O my brother, open and ye shall receive. Press on through the valley of darkness, overcome the dweller of night, keep ever thine eyes to the LIGHT-PLANE, and thou shalt be One with the LIGHT.

Man is in process of changing, to forms that are not of this world; grows he in time to the formless, a plane on the cycle above. Know ye, ye must become formless before ye are one with the LIGHT.

List ye, O man, to my voice, telling of pathways to Light, showing the way of attainment, when ye shall be one with the Light.

Search ye the mysteries of earth's heart, learn, of the LAW that exists, holding the stars in their balance, by the force of the primordial mist. Seek ye the flame of the EARTH'S LIFE, bathe in the glare of its flame, follow the three cornered pathway, until thou too art a flame.

Speak thou in words without voice, to those who dwell down below, enter the blue-litten Temple and bathe in the fire of all life.

Know, O man, thou art complex, a being of earth and of fire; let thy flame shine out brightly, be thou only the fire.

Wisdom is hidden in darkness, when lit by the flame of the Soul, find thou the wisdom and be LIGHT-BORN, a Sun of the Light, without form. Seek thee ever more wisdom, find it in heart of the flame, know that only by striving can Light pour into thy brain. Now have I spoken with wisdom, list to my Voice and obey, tear open the Veils of the darkness, shine a LIGHT on the WAY.

Speak I of Ancient Atlantis, speak of the days of the

Kingdom of Shadows, speak of the coming of the children of shadows. Out of the great deep were they called by the wisdom of earth-men, called for the purpose of gaining great power.

Far in the past before Atlantis existed, men there were who delved into darkness, using dark magic, calling up beings from the great deep below us. Forth came they into this cycle, formless were they, of another vibration, existing unseen by the children of earth-men. Only through blood could they have formed being, only through man could they live in the world.

In ages past were they conquered by the Masters, driven below to the place whence they came. But some there were who remained, hidden in spaces and planes unknown to man. Lived they in Atlantis as shadows, but at times they appeared among men. Aye, when the blood was offered, forth came they to dwell among men.

In the form of man moved they amongst us, but only to sight, were they as are men. Serpent-headed when the glamour was lifted, but appearing to man as men among men. Crept they into the Councils, taking forms that were like unto men. Slaying by their arts the chiefs of the kingdoms, taking their form and ruling o'er man. Only by magic, could they be discovered, only by sound could their faces be seen. Sought they from the kingdom of shadows, to destroy man and rule in his place.

But, know ye, the Masters were mighty in magic, able to lift the Veil from the face of the serpent, able to send him back to his place. Came they to man and taught him the secret, the Word that only a man can pronounce; swift then they lifted the Veil from the serpent, and cast him forth from place among men.

Yet, beware, the serpent still liveth, in a place that is open, at times, to the world. Unseen they walk among thee, in places where the rites have been said; again as time passes onward, shall they take the semblance of men.

Called, may they be, by the master who knows the white or the black, but only the white master may control and bind them while in the flesh.

Seek not the kingdom of shadows, for evil will surely appear, for only the master of brightness shall conquer the shadow of fear.

Know ye, O my brother, that fear is an obstacle great; be master of all in the brightness, the shadow will soon disappear. Hear ye, and heed my wisdom, the voice of LIGHT is clear, seek not the valley of shadow, and light only will appear.

List ye, O man, to the depth of my wisdom, speak I of knowledge hidden from man. Far have I been, on my journeys through SPACE-TIME, even to the end of the space of this cycle. Found I there the great barrier, holding man from leaving this cycle. Aye, glimpsed I the HOUNDS of the Barrier, lying in wait for he who would pass them. In that space, where time exists not, faintly I sensed the guardians of cycles. Move they, only through angles, free are they not of the curved dimensions.

Strange and terrible are the HOUNDS of the Barrier, follow they consciousness to the limits of space. Think not, to escape by entering your body, for follow they fast the Soul, through angles. Only the circle will give ye protection, save from the claws of the DWELLERS in ANGLES.

Once, in a time past, I approached the great Barrier, and saw on the shores where time exists not, the formless forms of the HOUNDS of the Barrier; aye, hiding in the mist beyond time I found them, and THEY, scenting me afar off, raised themselves and gave the great bell cry, that can be heard from cycle to cycle, and moved through space toward my Soul.

Fled I then, fast before them, back from times unthinkable end, but ever after me pursued they, moving in strange angles not known to man. Aye, on the gray shore of TIME-SPACES end found I the HOUNDS of the Barrier, ravening for the Soul who attempts the beyond.

Fled I, through circles back to my body, fled, and fast after me they followed. Aye, after me the devourers followed, seeking through angles to devour my Soul.

Aye, know ye man, that the Soul who dares the Barrier, may be held in bondage by the HOUNDS from beyond time, held till this cycle is all completed, and left behind when the consciousness leaves.

Entered I my body, created the circles that know not angles, created the form that from my form was formed, made my body into a circle, and lost the pursuers in the circles of time. But, even yet, when free from my body, cautious, ever, must I be not to move through angles, else my Soul might never be free.

Know ye, the HOUNDS of the Barrier move only through angles, and never through curves of space. Only by moving through curves can ye escape them, for in angles they will pursue thee. O man, heed ye my warning, seek not to break open the gate to beyond. Few there are who have succeeded in passing the Barrier, to the greater LIGHT that shines beyond. For know ye, ever the dwellers, seek such Souls to hold in their thrall.

Listen, O man, and heed ye my warning, seek ye to move not in angles, but curves, and if while free from thy body, thou hearest the sound like the bay of a hound, ringing clear and bell-like through thy being, flee back to thy body through circles, penetrate not the mist before.

When thou hast entered the form thou hast dwelt in, use thou the cross and the circle combined, open thy mouth and use thou thy Voice, utter the WORD and thou shalt be free. Only the one who, of LIGHT, has the fullest can hope to pass by the guards of the way, and then must he move through strange curves and angles, that are formed in direction not known to man.

List ye, O man, and heed ye my warning, attempt not to pass the guards in the way, rather should ye seek to gain of thine own light, and make thyself ready to pass on the way.

LIGHT is thine ultimate end, O my brother, seek and find ever the Light on thy way.

EMERALD TABLETS

TABLET IX

THE KEY TO FREEDOM
OF SPACE

List ye, O man, hear ye my voice, teaching of wisdom and light in this cycle; teaching ye how to banish the darkness, teaching ye how to bring light in thy life.

Seek ye, O man, to find the great pathway, that leads to eternal LIFE as a SUN. Draw ye away from the veil of the darkness, seek to become a Light in the world. Make of thyself a vessel for Light, a focus for the Sun of this space.

Lift thou thine eyes to the Cosmos, lift thou thine eyes to the Light, speak in the words of the Dweller, the chant that calls down the Light. Sing thou the song of freedom, sing thou the song of the Soul, create the high vibration that will make thee One with the Whole. Blend all thyself with the Cosmos, grow into ONE with the Light, be thou a channel of order, a pathway of LAW to the world.

Thy LIGHT, O man, is the great LIGHT, shining through the shadow of flesh, free must thou rise from the darkness, before thou art One with the LIGHT.

Shadows of darkness surround thee, life fills thee

with its flow, but know, O man, thou must arise and forth from thy body go, far to the planes that surround thee and yet are One with thee too.

Look all around thee, O man, see thine own light reflected, aye, even in the darkness around thee, thine own light pours forth through the veil.

Seek thou for wisdom always, let not thine body betray, keep in the path of the Light wave, shun thou the darkened way. Know thee that wisdom is lasting, existing since the ALL-SOUL began, creating harmony from chaos, by the law that exists in the WAY.

List ye, O man, to the teaching of wisdom, list to the voice that speaks of the past-time. Aye, I shall tell thee of knowledge forgotten, tell ye of wisdom hidden in past-time, lost in the mist of darkness around me.

Know ye, man, ye are the ultimate of all things only the knowledge of this is forgotten, lost when man was cast into bondage, bound and fettered by the chains of the darkness.

Long, long ago, I cast off my body, wandered I free through the vastness of ether, circled the angles that hold man in bondage. Know ye, O man, ye are only a spirit, the body is nothing, the Soul is the All. Let not your body be a fetter, cast off the darkness and travel in Light. Cast off your body, O man, and be free, truly a Light that is ONE with the Light.

When ye are free from the fetters of darkness, and travel in space, as a SUN of the LIGHT, then ye shall know that space is not boundless, but truly bounded by angles and curves. Know ye, O man, that all that exists, is only an aspect of greater things yet to come. Matter is fluid and flows like a stream, constantly changing from One thing to another.

All through the ages has knowledge existed, never been changed, though buried in darkness, never been lost, though forgotten by man.

Know ye, that throughout the space that ye dwell in, are others as great as your own, interlaced through the heart of your matter, yet separate in space of their own.

Once in a time long forgotten, I, THOTH, opened the doorway, penetrated into other spaces, and learned of the secrets concealed. Deep in the essence of matter are many mysteries concealed.

Nine are the interlocked dimensions, and nine are the cycles of space, nine are the diffusions of consciousness, and nine are the worlds within worlds, aye, nine are the Lords of the cycles that come from above and below.

Space is filled with concealed ones, for space is divided by time, seek ye the key to the time-space, and ye shall unlock the gate. Know ye that throughout the time-space consciousness surely exists, though from our knowledge it is hidden, yet still it forever exists.

The key to worlds within thee, are found only within, for man is the gateway of mystery, and the key that is One within One.

Seek ye within the circle, use the WORD I shall give, open the gateway within thee and surely thou too shalt live. Man, ye think that ye liveth, but know it is life within death, for as sure as ye are bound to your body, for you no life exists. Only the Soul that is space-free, has life that is really a life; all else is only a bondage, a fetter from which to be free.

Think not that man is earth-born, though come from the earth he may be, man is a light-born spirit, but, without knowing, he can never be free. Darkness surrounds the light-born, darkness fetters the Soul, only the one who is seeking, may ever hope to be free.

Shadows around thee are falling, darkness fills all the space, shine forth, O LIGHT of the man-soul, fill thou the darkness of space.

Ye are a SUN of the GREAT LIGHT, remember and ye shall be free, stay not thou in the shadows, spring forth from the darkness of night. Light, let thy Soul be, O SUN-BORN, filled with glory of Light, freed from the bonds of the darkness, a Soul that is One with the Light.

Thou art the key to all wisdom, within thee is all time and space, live not in bondage to darkness, free thou thy Light-form from night.

"Great Light, that fills all the Cosmos, flow thou fully to man, make of his body a light-torch, that shall never be quenched among men."

Long in the past, sought I wisdom, knowledge not known to man. Far to the past I traveled, into the space where time began. Sought I ever new knowledge, to add to the wisdom I knew, yet only I found did the future hold the key to the wisdom I sought.

Down to the HALLS of AMENTI I journeyed, the greater knowledge to seek, asked of the LORDS of the CYCLES, the way to the wisdom I sought. Asked the LORDS this question: "Where is the source of ALL?" Answered, in tones that were mighty, the voice of the LORD of the NINE, "Free thou thy Soul from thy body, and come forth with me to the LIGHT."

Forth I came from my body, a glittering flame in the night, stood I before the LORDS, bathed in the fire of LIFE. Seized was I then by a force, great beyond knowledge of man, cast was I to the Abyss, through spaces unknown to man.

Saw I the moulding of order, from the chaos and angles of night, saw I the LIGHT spring from order, and heard the voice of the Light. Saw I the flame of the Abyss, casting forth order and light, saw order spring out of chaos, saw Light giving forth Life.

Then heard I the voice, "Hear thou and understand, the flame is the source of all things, containing all things in potentiality, the order that sent forth light is the WORD, and from the WORD comes LIFE, and the existence of all." And again spoke the voice, saying: "The LIFE in thee is the WORD, find thou the LIFE within thee, and have powers to use of the WORD."

Long I watched the Light-flame, pouring forth from the Essence of Fire, realizing that LIFE is but order, and that man is one with the fire.

Back I came to my body, stood again with the Nine, listened to the voice of the CYCLES, vibrate with powers they spoke; "Know ye, O Thoth, that LIFE, is but the WORD of the FIRE, the LIFE force ye see before thee, is but the WORD in the World as a fire. Seek ye the path to the WORD, and powers shall surely be thine."

Then asked I of the Nine, "O Lord, show me the path, give me the path to the wisdom, show me the way to the WORD." Answered, me then, the LORD of the NINE, "Through ORDER ye shall find the way. Saw ye not that the WORD came from Chaos, saw ye not that LIGHT came from FIRE? Look in thy life for disorder, balance and order thy life, quell all the Chaos of emotions and thou shalt have order in LIFE. ORDER brought forth from Chaos will bring thee the WORD of the SOURCE, will give thee the power of CYCLES, and make of thy Soul a force, that free, will extend through the ages, a perfected SUN from the SOURCE."

Listened I to the voice, and deep sank the words in my heart, for ever have I sought for order, that I might draw on the WORD. Know ye that he who attains it must ever in ORDER be, for use of the WORD through disorder, has never, and can never be.

Take ye these words, O man, as part of thy life, let them be, seek thee to conquer disorder, and One with the WORD thou shalt be.

Put forth thy effort in gaining LIGHT, on the pathway of Life, seek to be One with the SUN-STATE, seek to be solely the LIGHT. Hold thou thy thought on the Oneness of light with the body of man, know that all is order, from Chaos, born into Light.

EMERALD TABLETS

TABLET X

THE KEY OF TIME

List ye, O man, take of my wisdom, learn of the deep hidden mysteries of space. Learn of the THOUGHT that grew in the abyss, bringing order and harmony in space.

Know ye, O man, that all that exists, has being only because of the Law. Know ye, the LAW and ye shall be free, never be bound by the fetters of night.

Far, through strange spaces, have I journeyed, into the depth of the abyss of time, learning strange and yet stranger mysteries, until in the end all was revealed. Know ye, that mystery is only mystery, when it is knowledge unknown to man; when ye have plumbed the heart of all mystery, knowledge and wisdom will surely be thine.

Seek ye, and learn that TIME is the secret, whereby ye may be free of this space.

Long have I, THOTH, sought wisdom, aye, and shall seek to eternity's end, for know I that ever before me receding, shall move the goal I seek to attain. Even the LORDS of the CYCLES know that not yet have THEY reached the goal, for with all of their wisdom, they know that TRUTH ever grows.

Once in a past time, I spoke to the Dweller, asked of

the mystery of time and space; asked him the question, that surged in my being, saying: "O master, what is time?"

Then to me spoke HE, the master, "Know ye, O Thoth, in the beginning there was VOID and nothingness, a timeless, spaceless, nothingness. And into the nothingness came a thought, purposeful, all pervading, and IT filled the VOID. There existed no matter, only force, a movement, a vortex or vibration of the purposeful thought that filled the VOID."

And I questioned the master, saying: "Was this thought eternal?" And answered me the DWELLER, saying: "In the beginning there was eternal thought, and for thought to be eternal, time must exist, so into the all pervading thought grew the LAW OF TIME. Aye, time which exists through all space, flowing in a smooth rhythmic movement, that is eternally in a state of fixation, Time changes not, but all things change in time, for time is the force that holds events separate, each in its proper place. Time is not in motion but ye move through time as your consciousness moves from one event to another. Aye, by time ye exist, all in all, an eternal ONE existence. Know ye, that even though in time ye are separate, yet still are ye ONE in all time existent." Ceased then the voice of the Dweller, and departed I to ponder on time. For knew I, that in these words, lay wisdom and a way to explore the mysteries of time.

Of't did I ponder the words of the Dweller, then sought I to solve the mystery of time. Found I that time moves through strange angles. Yet only by curves could I hope to attain the key, that would give me access to the time-space. Found I that only by moving upward, and yet again by moving to right-ward, could I be free from the time of this movement.

Forth I came from out of my body, moved in the movements that changed me in time. Strange were the sights I saw in my journeys, many the mysteries that opened to view. Aye, saw I man's beginning, learned from the past that nothing is new.

Seek ye, O man, to learn the pathway that leads through the spaces that are formed forth in time.

Forget not, O man, with all of thy seeking, that light is the goal, ye shall seek to attain. Search ye ever for light on thy pathway, and ever for thee the goal shall endure. Let not thine heart turn, ever to darkness, light let thine Soul be, a Sun on the way. Know ye, that in the eternal brightness, ye shall ever find thy Soul hid in light, never fettered by bondage to darkness, ever it shines forth a Sun of the Light.

Aye, know though hidden in darkness, your Soul, a spark of the true flame, exists. Be ye ONE, with the greatest of all lights, find at the SOURCE, the END of thy goal.

Light is life, for without the great light nothing can ever exist. Know ye, that in all formed matter the heart of light always exists, aye, even though bound in the darkness, inherent light always exists.

Once I stood in the HALLS of AMENTI, and heard the voice of the LORDS of AMENTI, saying in tones that rang through the silence, words of power, mighty and potent. Chanted they the song of the cycles, the words that opened the path to beyond. Aye, I saw the great path opened and looked for an instant into the beyond. Saw I, the movements of the cycles; vast as the thought of the SOURCE could convey.

Knew I then that even infinity, is moving on to some unthinkable end. Saw I, that the Cosmos is order, and part of a movement that extends to all space, a part of an order of orders, constantly moving in a harmony of space. Saw I, the wheeling of cycles, like vast circles across the sky, knew I then that all that has being, is growing to meet yet other being. In a far off grouping of space and of time. Knew I then that in Words are power, to open the planes that are hidden from man. Aye, that even in Words, lies hidden the key that will open above and below.

Hark ye, now man, this word I leave with thee, use it and ye shall find power in its sound. Say ye, the word: "ZIN-URU" and power shall ye find, yet must ye understand that man is of light, and light is of man.

List ye, O man, and hear a mystery, stranger than all that lies neath the Sun. Know ye, O man, that all space is filled by worlds within worlds, aye, one within the other, yet separate by law.

Once in my search for deep buried wisdom, I opened the door that bars THEM from man, called I from other planes of being, one who was fairer than the daughters of men. Aye, I called her from out of the spaces to shine as a light in the world of men.

Used I the drum of the Serpent, wore I the robe of the purple and gold, placed on my head I, the crown of Silver, around me the circle of cinnabar, shone. Raised I my arms and cried the invocation that opens the path to the planes beyond; cried to the LORDS of the SIGNS, in their houses, "Lords of the two horizons, watchers of the treble gates, stand ye One at the right, and One at the left, as the STAR rises to his throne and rules over his sign. Aye, thou dark prince of ARULU, open the gates of the dim hidden land, and release her whom ye keep imprisoned.

"Hear ye, hear ye, hear ye, dark Lords and shining Ones, and by their secret names, names, which I know and can pronounce, hear ye and obey my will."

Lit I then with flame my circle, and called to HER in the space-planes beyond. Daughter of Light return from ARULU. Seven times and seven times have I passed through the fire; food have I not eaten, water have I not drunk. I call thee from ARULU, from the realm of EKER-SHEGAL, I summon thee, Lady of Light.

Then before me rose the dark figures, aye, the figures of the Lords of ARULU, parted they before me and forth came the Lady of Light. Free was she now from the LORDS of the night, free to live in the light of the earth Sun, free to live as a child of Light.

Hear ye, and listen, O my children, magic is knowledge and only is Law. Be not afraid of the power within thee, for it follows law as the stars in the sky.

Know ye, that to he without knowledge, wisdom is magic, and not of the Law; but know ye, that ever ye by your knowledge can approach closer to a place in the Sun.

List ye, my children, follow my teaching, be ye ever seeker of light, shine in the world of men all around thee, a light on the path that shall shine among men.

Follow ye, and learn of my magic, know that all force is thine if thou wilt. Fear not the path that leads thee to knowledge, but rather shun ye, the dark road.

Light is thine, O man, for the taking, cast off the fetters and thou shalt be free. Know ye, that thy Soul is living in bondage fettered by fear that holds ye in thrall. Open thy eyes and see the great SUN-LIGHT, be not afraid for all is thine own. Fear is the LORD of dark ARULU, to he who has never faced the dark fear. Aye, know that fear has existence, created by those who are bound by their fears.

Shake off thy bondage, O children, and walk in the light of the glorious day. Never turn thy thoughts to the darkness and surely ye shall be One with the Light.

Man is only what he believeth, a brother of darkness or a child of the Light. Come thou into the light my Children, walk in the pathway that leads to the Sun.

Hark ye, now and list to the wisdom, use thou the word I have given unto thee, use it and surely thou shalt find power and wisdom, and light to walk in the way. Seek thee and find the key I have given, and ever shalt thou be a Child of the Light.

EMERALD TABLETS

TABLET XI

THE KEY TO ABOVE AND BELOW

Hear ye, and list ye, O children of KHEM, to the words that I give that shall bring ye to light. Ye know, O men, that I knew your fathers, aye, your fathers in a time long ago. Deathless have I been through all the ages, living among ye since your knowledge began. Leading ye upward to the Light of the Great Soul, have I ever striven, drawing ye from out of the darkness of night.

Know ye, O people amongs't whom I walk, that I, Thoth, have all of the knowledge, and all of the wisdom, known to man since the ancient days. Keeper have I been of the secrets of the great race, holder of the key that leads into life. Bringer up have I been to ye, O my children, even from the darkness of the Ancient of Days. List ye now, to the words of my wisdom, list ye now, to the message I bring. Hear ye now the word I give thee, and ye shall be raised from the darkness to Light.

Far in the past, when first I came to thee, found I thee in caves of rocks. Lifted I thee by my power and wisdom, until thou dids't shine as men among men. Aye, found I thee without any knowing, only a little were ye raised beyond beasts. Fanned I ever the spark of thy consciousness, until at last ye flamed as men.

Now shall I speak to thee of knowledge, ancient beyond the thought of thy race. Know ye that we of the Great Race had, and have knowledge, that is more than man's. Wisdom we gained from the star-born races, wisdom and knowledge far beyond man's. Down to us had descended masters of wisdom, as far beyond us as I am from thee. List ye, now while I give ye wisdom, use it and free shalt thou be.

Know ye that in the pyramid I builded are the KEYS that shall show ye the WAY into life; aye, draw ye a line from the great image, I builded, to the apex of the pyramid, built as a gateway. Draw ye another opposite in the same angle and direction, dig ye and find that which I have hidden. There shall ye find the underground entrance, to the secrets hidden before ye were men.

Tell ye, I now of the mystery of cycles, that move in movements that are strange to the finite, for infinite are they beyond knowledge of man. Know ye that there are nine of the cycles, aye, nine above and fourteen below; moving in harmony to the place of joining, that shall exist in the future of time. Know ye that the LORDS of the CYCLES are units of consciousness, sent from the others to unify THIS with the ALL. Highest are THEY of the consciousness of all of the CYCLES, working in harmony with the LAW. Know THEY, that in time all will be perfected, having none above and none below, but all ONE in a perfected infinity, a harmony of all in the ONENESS of ALL.

Deep neath earth's surface in the HALLS of

AMENTI, sit the Seven, the LORDS of the CYCLES, aye, and another, the Lord from below. Yet know thee, that in infinity there is neither above nor below. But ever there is, and ever shall be. ONENESS of ALL when all is complete. Oft have I journeyed to the HALLS of AMENTI, oft have I stood before the LORDS of the ALL. Oft at the fount of their wisdom have drunken, and filled both my body and Soul with their Light.

Spake they to me and told me of cycles, and the LAW that gives them the means to exist. Aye, spake to me the LORD of the NINE, saying: "O Thoth, great are ye among earth's children but mysteries exist of which ye know not. Ye know that ye came from a space-time below this, and know ye shall travel to a space-time beyond; but little ye know of the mysteries within them, little ye know of the wisdom beyond. Know ye, that ye, as a whole in this consciousness, are only a cell in the process of growth.

"The consciousness below thee is ever expanding, in different ways from those known to thee. Aye, it, though in space-time below thee, is ever growing in ways that are different, from those that were part of the ways of thine own. For know that it grows as a result of thy growth, but not in the same way that thou didst grow. The growth that thou had, and have in the present, have brought into being a cause and effect. No consciousness follows the path of those before it, else all would be repetition and vain. Each consciousness in the cycle it exists in, follows its own path to the ultimate goal. Each plays its part in the Plan of the Cosmos; each plays its part in the ultimate end. The farther the cycle, the greater its knowledge and ability to blend the law of the whole.

"Know ye, that ye in the cycles below us are working the minor parts of the Law, while we of the cycle that extends to infinity take of thy striving, and build greater Law.

"Each has his own part to play in the cycles, each has his work to complete, in his way. The cycle below thee, is yet not below thee, but only formed for a need that exists. For know ye, that the fountain of wisdom, that sends forth the cycles, is eternally seeking new powers to gain. Ye know that knowledge is gained only by practice, and wisdom comes forth only from knowledge, and thus are the cycles created by Law. Means are they for the gaining of knowledge, for the Plane of Law that is the Source of the ALL. The cycle below is not truly below but only different in space and in time. The consciousness there, is working and testing lesser things, than those ye are; and know just as ye are working on greater, so above ye are those who are also working, as ye are, on yet other laws. The difference that exists between the cycles, is only in ability to work with the law. We, who have being in cycles beyond thee, are those who first came forth from the SOURCE, and have, in the passage through time-space, gained ability to use laws of the Greater, that are far beyond the conception of man. Nothing there is, that is really below thee, but only a different operation of Law.

"Look thee above, or look thee below, the same shall

ye find, for all is but part of the Oneness that is at the Source of the Law. The consciousness below thee is part thine own, as we are a part of thine.

"Ye, as a child had not the knowledge that came to ye when ye became a man. Compare ye the cycles to man in his journey from birth unto death, and see in the cycle below thee, the child with the knowledge he has, and see ye yourself as the child grown older, advancing in knowledge as time passes on, see ye, WE, also, as the child grown to manhood, with the knowledge and wisdom that came with the years. So also, O Thoth, are the cycles of consciousness, children in different stages of growth, yet all from the one Source, the Wisdom, and all to the Wisdom returning again." Ceased then HE from speaking, and sat in the silence that comes to the LORDS. Then again spake HE unto me, saying: "O Thoth, long have WE sat in Amenti, guarding the flame of life in the Halls. Yet know, we are still part of our Cycles, with our Vision reaching unto them and beyond. Aye, know we that of all, nothing else matters, excepting the growth we can gain with our Soul; know we the flesh is fleeting, the things men count great are nothing to us. The things we seek are not of the body, but are only the perfected state of the Soul. When ye, as men, can learn that nothing but progress of Soul can count in the end, then truly ye are free from all bondage, free to work in a harmony of Law.

"Know, O man, ye should aim at perfection, for only thus can ye attain to the goal. Though ye should know that nothing is perfect, yet it should be thy aim and thy goal."

Ceased again the voice of the Nine, and into my consciousness the words had sunk. Now, seek I ever more wisdom that I may be perfect in Law with the all.

Soon go I down to the Halls of Amenti, to live neath the cold flower of life. Ye whom I have taught shall never more see me, yet live I, forever, in the wisdom I taught.

All that man is, is because of his wisdom, all that he shall be is the result of his cause.

List ye, now to my voice and become greater than common man. Lift thine eyes upward, let light fill thy being, be thou ever Children of Light. Only by effort shall ye grow upward to the plane where light is the All of the All. Be ye the master of all that surrounds thee, never be mastered by the effects of thy life. Create then ever more perfect causes, and in time shalt thou be a Sun of the Light.

Free, let thine soul soar, ever upward, free from the bondage and fetters of night. Lift thine eyes to the Sun in the sky-space, for thee, let it be a symbol of life. Know that thou art the Great Light, perfect in thine own sphere, when thou art free. Look not ever into the blackness, lift up thine eyes to the spaces above, free let thine light flame upward, and shalt thou be a Child of the LIGHT.

EMERALD TABLETS

TABLET XII

THE LAW OF CAUSE AND EFFECT AND THE KEY OF PROPHESY

List ye, O man, to the words of my wisdom, list to the voice of Thoth, the Atlantean. Conquered have I the law of the time-space, knowledge have I gained of the future of time. Know I that man in his movement through space-time, shall ever be ONE with the ALL.

Know ye, O man, that all of the future is an open book to him who can read. All effect shall bring forth its causes, as all effects grew from the first cause. Know ye, the future is not fixed or stable, but varies as cause brings forth an effect. Look in the cause thou shalt bring into being, and surely thou shalt see that all is effect.

In the great beginning there grew the first cause, that brought into being all that exists. Thou, thyself, art the effect of causation, and in turn are the cause of yet other effects.

So, O man, be sure the effects that ye bring forth, are ever causes of more perfect effects. Know ye the future is never in fixation, but follows man's free will as it moves through the movements of time-space, toward the goal where a new time begins. Man can only read the future through the causes that bring the effects. Seek ye within causation and surely ye shall find the effects.

List ye, O man, while I speak of the future, speak of the effect that follows the cause. Know ye that man in his journey light-ward is ever seeking escape from the night. Aye, from the blackness of night that surrounds him, like the shadows that surround the stars in the sky, and like the stars in the sky-space, he too, shall shine from the shadows of night.

Ever his destiny shall lead him onward, until he is ONE with the Light; aye, though his way lies mids't the shadows, ever before him glows the Great Light. Dark though the way be, yet shall he conquer the shadows that flow around him like night.

Far in the future I see men as light-born, free from the darkness that fetters the Soul, living in light, without the bonds of the darkness to cover the light, that is light of their Soul. Know ye, O man, before ye attain this, that many the dark shadows shall fall on your light, striving to quench with shadows of darkness, the light of the Soul that strives to be free.

Great is the struggle between light and darkness, age old and yet ever new. Yet know in a time, far in the future, light shall be all, and darkness shall fall.

List ye, O man, to my words of wisdom, prepare and ye shall not bind your light. Man has risen, and man has fallen, as ever new waves of consciousness flow, from the great abyss below us, toward the Sun of their goal.

Ye, my children, have risen from a state that was little above the beast, until now of all men ye are greatest yet before thee, were others greater than thee. Yet tell I thee as before thee, others have fallen, so also shall ye come to an end, and upon the land where ye dwell now, barbarians shall dwell, and in turn rise to Light. Forgotten shall be the ancient wisdom, yet ever shall live, though hidden from men.

Aye, in the land thou callest Khem, races shall rise and races shall fall, forgotten shalt thou be of the children of men. Yet thou shalt have moved to a star-space beyond this, leaving behind this place where thou hast dwelt.

The Soul of man moves ever onward, bound not by any one star. But ever moving to the great goal before him, where he is dissolved in the Light of the All. Know ye, that ye shall ever go onward, moved by the law of cause and effect, until in the end, both become One.

Aye, man, after ye have gone, others shall move in the places ye lived; knowledge and wisdom shall all be forgotten, and only a memory of Gods shall survive. As I to thee am a God, by my knowledge, so ye too shall be Gods of the future, because of your knowledge far above theirs. Yet know ye, that all through the ages, man shall have access to Law when he will.

Ages to come shall see revival of wisdom, to those who shall inherit thy place on this star, they shall in turn come into wisdom, and learn to banish the darkness by Light. Yet greatly must they strive through the ages, to bring into themselves the freedom of Light. Many who are bound in darkness shall strive to hold others from

Light; then shall there come unto man the great warfare, that shall make the earth tremble and shake in its course, aye, then shall the Dark Brothers open the warfare between Light and the Night.

When man again shall conquer the ocean, and fly in the air on wings like the birds, when he has learned to harness the lightning, then shall the time of warfare begin. Great shall the battle be twixt the forces, great the warfare of darkness and light. Nation shall rise against nation, using the dark forces to shatter the earth. Weapons of force shall wipe out the Earth-men, until half of the races of men shall be gone. Then shall come forth the Sons of the Morning, and give their edict to the children of men, saying: "O men, cease from thy striving against thy brother, only thus can ye come to the Light. Cease from thy unbelief, O my brother, and follow the path and know ye are right."

Then shall men cease from their striving, brother against brother, and father against son. Then shall the ancient home of my people, rise from its place neath the dark ocean waves. Then shall the age of Light be unfolded, with all men seeking the Light of the goal. Then shall the Brothers of Light rule the people, banished shall be the darkness of night.

Aye, the children of men shall progress, onward and upward to the great goal, children of Light shall they become, flame of the flame, shall their Souls ever be. Knowledge and wisdom shall be man's, in the great age, for he shall approach the eternal flame, the SOURCE of all wisdom; the place of beginning, that is yet ONE with the end of all things. Aye, in a time that is yet unborn, all shall be ONE and ONE shall be all. Man, a perfect flame of this Cosmos, shall move forward to a place in the stars. Aye, shall move, even from out of this space-time, into another beyond the stars.

Long have ye listened to me, O my children, long have ye listened to the wisdom of Thoth. Now I depart from ye, into darkness; now go I, to the HALLS of AMENTI, there to dwell until in the future, light shall come again to man. Yet, know ye, my Spirit shall ever be with thee, guiding thy feet in the pathway of Light.

Guard ye the secrets I leave with thee, and surely my spirit will guard thee through life. Keep thine eyes ever on the pathway to wisdom, keep the Light as thy goal ever-more. Fetter not thy Soul in bondage of darkness; free, let it wing in its flight to the stars.

Now I depart from thee, to dwell in Amenti, be thou my children, in this life and the next. The time will come when ye, too, shall be deathless; living from age to age, a light among men.

Guard ye the entrance to the HALLS of AMENTI, Guard ye the secrets I have hidden among ye, let not the wisdom be cast to barbarians, secret shall thou keep it, for those who seek Light. Now depart I, receive thou my blessing, take thou my way and follow the Light.

Blend thou thy Soul in the Great Essence, ONE with the Great Light, let thy consciousness be. Call thou on me when thou dost need me, use thou my name three times in a row: Chequetet, Arelich, Vomalites.

EMERALD TABLETS

TABLET XIII

THE KEYS OF LIFE AND DEATH

List ye, O man, Hear ye the wisdom, Hear ye the Word that shall fill thee with Life. Hear ye, the Word that shall banish the darkness, Hear ye, the voice that shall banish the night.

Mystery and wisdom, have I brought to my children, Knowledge and power descended from old. Know ye not that all shall be opened, when ye shall find the oneness of all? One shall ye be with the Masters of Mystery, Conquerors of Death and Masters of Life. Aye, ye shall learn of the flower of Amenti, the blossom of life that shines in the Halls. In Spirit shall ye reach the Halls of Amenti, and bring back the wisdom that liveth in Light. Know ye, the gateway to power is secret, Know ye, the gateway to life is through death. Aye, through death, but not as ye know death, but a death that is life, and is fire and is light.

Desireth thou to know the deep hidden secret? Look in thy heart where the knowledge is bound. Know that in thee the secret is hidden, the source of all life, and the source of all death.

List ye, O man, while I tell the secret, reveal unto thee, the secret of old.

Deep in earth's heart lies the flower, the source of the Spirit that binds all in its form. For know ye that the earth is living in body as thou art alive in thine own formed form. The flower of life is as thine own place of Spirit, and streams through the earth as thine flows through thy form. Giving of life to the earth and its children, renewing the Spirit from form unto form. This is the Spirit that is form of thy body, shaping and molding into its form.

Know ye, O man, that thy form is dual, balanced in polarity while formed in its form. Know that when fast on thee, DEATH approaches, it is only because thy balance is shaken, it is only because one pole has been lost.

Know that thy body when in perfect balance, may never be touched by the finger of DEATH. Aye, even accident, may only approach when the balance is gone. When ye are in a balanced equilibrium, ye shall live on in time, and not taste of Death. Know that thou art the balanced completion, existing because of thy balance of poles. As in thee one pole is drawn downward, fast from thee goes the balance of life, then unto thee cold Death approaches, and change must come to thine unbalanced life.

Know that the secret of life in AMENTI is the secret of restoring the balance of poles. All that exists, has form and is living because of the Spirit of life in its poles.

See ye not, that in earth's heart is the balance of all things that exist, and have being on its face. The source of thy Spirit is drawn from earth's heart—for in thy form thou art one with the earth.

When thou hast learned to hold thine own balance,

then shalt thou draw on the balance of earth. Exist then shalt thou, while earth is existing, changing in form only, when earth too shalt change. Tasting not of death, but one with this planet, holding thy form till all pass away.

List ye, O man, whilst I give the secret, so that ye too shalt taste not of change. One hour each day shalt thou lie with thine head pointed to the place of the positive pole, (north), one hour each day shalt thy head be pointed to the place of the negative pole (south). Whilst thy head is placed to the northward hold thou thy consciousness from the chest to the head and when thy head is placed to the southward hold thou thy thought from the chest to the feet. Hold thou in balance once in each seven and thy balance will retain the whole of its strength. Aye, if thou be old, thy body will freshen, and thy strength will become as a youth's. This is the secret, known to the Masters, by which they hold off the fingers of Death. Neglect not to follow the path I have shown, for when thou hast passed beyond years to a hundred to neglect it will mean the coming of Death.

Hear ye, my words, and follow this pathway. Keep thou thy balance and live on in life.

Hear ye, O man, and list to my voice, list to the wisdom that gives thee of Death. When at the end of thy work appointed, thou may desire to pass from this life, pass to the plane where the Suns of the Morning live and have being as Children of Light; pass without pain and pass without sorrow, into the plane where is eternal light.

First lie at rest with thine head to the eastward, fold

thou thy hands at the Source of thy life (solar plexus), place thou thy consciousness in the life seat, whirl it and divide to north and to south. Send thou the one out toward the northward, send thou the other out to the south. Relax thou thy hold upon thy being, forth from thy form will thy silver spark fly. Upward and onward to the Sun of the morning, blending with light, at one with its source. There it shall flame till desire shall be created, then shall return to a place in a form. Know ye, O men, that thus pass the great Souls, changing at will from life unto life. Thus ever, passes the Avatar, willing his Death as he wills his own life.

The key to the placing of consciousness at the time of Death so that Memory may be carried from one incarnation to another.

List ye, O man, drink of my wisdom, learn ye the secret, that is Master of TIME. Learn ye how those ye call Masters, are able to remember the lives of the past. Great is the secret yet easy to master, giving to thee the mastery of time. When upon thee death fast approaches, fear not but know ye are master of Death. Relax thy body, resist not with tension, place in thy heart the flame of thy Soul, swiftly then sweep it to the seat of the triangle, hold for a moment then move to the goal, this thy goal is the place between thine eyebrows, the place where the memory of life must hold sway. Hold thou thy flame here in thy brain-seat until the fingers of Death grasp thy Soul. Then as thou pass through the state of transition, surely the memories of life shall pass too. Then shall the past be as one with the present, then shall the memory of all be retained. Free shalt thou be from all retrogression, the things of the past shall live in today.

Man, ye have heard the voice of my wisdom, follow and ye shall live—through the ages as I.

* * * * * * * * * *

ADDITIONAL INFORMATION ON THE SECRETS OF ATLANTIS AND ITS TIME BY DR. DOREAL

SECRETS OF ATLANTIS

BY DR. DOREAL

By a great many people Atlantis is looked on as a legendary continent which never had real existence. The only account we have of Atlantis is the one by Plato in his "Dialogue with Timeaus", where he says his Grandfather was told by the Egyptian priests that their ancestors came from a land in the Western Ocean. This was supposed to have been destroyed by the sinking of the land some 12,000 years before.

It is true that few traces of their culture can be found today, but the Atlanteans left records that are still preserved by the Wisdom Schools.

The sinking of Atlantis was the source of the Universal legends of a deluge as recorded in the Old Testament, and in the folklore of almost every race in the World.

The ancient records of Atlantis tell us that the sinking of Atlantis was brought about because the souls of the Atlanteans who had developed such a tremendous knowledge about the cosmic and natural laws had passed on to a higher plane. Atlanteans of the last days were mostly souls that were low in the scale of development, yet they had access to the mighty science developed by their ancestors. This science was so great that if used improperly, it could have destroyed the World.

The people had deteriorated until they were no longer worthy to have access to the vast knowledge and wisdom that they had inherited from their ancestors. The souls that occupied the bodies of those in a later period of the Atlantean Age were souls that were low in development.

By the end of the Atlantean Age great advances had been made in the sciences and the arts. For instance they had developed flying machines that were capable of tremendous speeds, able to fly to the moon and back, and encircle the world in an hour or less. These ships were of a very light metal, similar to aluminum, but much harder than steel; they were very magnetic and susceptible to the magnetic currents of earth and of space. They were made of an alloy obtained by the action of sodium on sesqui-chloride of chromium subjected to electrical and magnetic stress. They were not effected by heat or cold, and even at cruising speed, capable of traveling a thousand miles an hour or more. They were powered by a helix of seven wires, the central one the greatest in diameter. Each alternate one was coiled in an opposite direction. These were collectors of magnetic current. Two twelve-foot antenna on the outside of the ship were connected to the wires of two helixes. These wires extended to the inner wall of the ship and were coiled in opposite directions around the ship over its entire length. The seven wires of each standard extended in radiation; those of one crossing those of the others, and were wound around the entire body of the ship as a core, which could be turned or moved in any direction on bearings. The current could be slowed or speeded up in its movement through these coils, thus advancing or retarding the speed of the ship or its distance from the earth. Each ship projected around itself a field force which prevented friction of the air from acting upon the ship. Also, through the use of their advanced science, they were able to suspend the gravity within the ship so that those who were on it were not effected by the tremendous speeds that it attained. With such ships, sailing vessels on the seas were unnecessary for they were able to go to their far flung colonies very quickly and without effort on their part.

The buildings of Atlantis, as of their colonies, were not composed of bricks and stones and metal, as of those of later date, but were created by fixing patterns of force in suspension and attracting around them vortices of cosmic dust. By the use of complicated patterns they were able to form or create great buildings in a matter of seconds and these remained intact until the pattern around which they were formed was dissolved by the builders. It is for this reason that we do not find monumental remains of the Ancient Atlanteans in the various parts of the world where their colonies had been built. When the Atlanteans passed, so also the patterns which they had set up, were dissolved and their buildings. The great cities vanished from the face of the earth with the exception of a few artifacts which had been created from the natural materials of the earth as hobbies by those who desired to maintain some of the arts of ancient times.

They had twelve months of twenty-eight days, and one of twenty-nine, for three years, and every fourth year one of thirty.

Their religion was the adoration of the principle of spiritual life which they called Den-Ze-Men-Ze. The priests were called the Deltsanza.

Punishment for crimes against the state was invariably exile from the Motherland and her colonies for varying periods of time.

There was a complete equality of sexes in civil life. Any

person of any age or sex being able to hold office in any of the positions either of the civil government or of the priestly caste.

Education was free but compulsory for all, for it was considered that one who did not have knowledge could not live life to its fullest. Their philosophy encompassed time, space, and life, three infinitely related elements cooperating eternal, immaterial, unchanging, in their relative condition of cooperation or co-dependence on the infinite cycle of existence.

The basic principles of their belief included the over-spirit, the source of animation, the immaterial form covering the spiritual, the material form covering the immaterial, the magnetic principle in universal creation, the electric principle in universal creation, the Infinite mind manifest in time, space, and light, the developing principle in universal creation. They taught that nothing exists without an infinite counterpart and nothing comes into existence without the ruling of specific natural law.

On one of the Islands was a great temple built in the form of a pyramid. This was on the Island called Unal. It was beneath this temple that the Halls of Amenti, which are spoken of in the Emerald Tablets, was found, and it was there that the seven Lords of the Cycles had their manifestation. This temple was not a temple of worship in the strictest sense of the word, but rather it was a focal point upon this earth of all of the Divine Wisdom of the Cosmic Consciousness or God.

There was another Island called Undal, upon which the great mystery schools were formed and it was there that all of those who passed beyond the ordinary schools of Atlantis went for instruction in the great mysteries of Light and the

Spirit. And it was there that the wise men of other races and nations of the earth came for instructions according as they were able to receive, to carry back to their own countries and peoples, knowledge and wisdom which later on was incorporated into the folklore and mythology of the descendants. Those races have been forgotten by present day man.

Beneath the earth the same Islands were inhabited by the Serpent Race with the bodies of man and the heads of great serpents. These serpents had the hypnotic power of causing their heads to assume that of any human being or form. Thus in the latter days, though they had been almost destroyed and exterminated by the great Atlantean race, the few survivors gradually began to insinuate themselves into the places of the rulers of Atlantis, killing them and assuming their form and features so that it became necessary for a means to be developed attesting as to whether one were a true man or the serpent race. The wise men evolved a word which could only be pronounced by human vocal cords and not by those of the snake people. That word was Kinninigan, and it is still a great dispeller of illusion. Once each year the rulers of Atlantis stood before the people assembled and pronounced the word so that people could know that they were ruled by their own kind. It is from the knowledge of the hypnotic power of the serpent race and their battle against mankind that we have the legends of warfare between man and the old serpents. And the legends that the serpent has hypnotic power. It was not the snake that we have today but the serpent that walks like a man. The old serpent race of Atlantis that man considered the ultimate of evil, gave rise to the legend of the serpent tempting Adam and Eve in the garden of Eden.

The wise men of Atlantis had developed great powers and forces which are unknown at the present time. In them the third eye was open. The greater part of the people could communicate with each other through the means of telepathy. They had knowledge of the molding force of creation which they used in the construction of their buildings and implements. That force was called Zuril, the molding force of creation.

The Atlanteans had great libraries in which books recording the history of a half million years could be found, but those books are not like the books which we read today, they were very small boxes. Each one with a small lens in it, a series of projecting studs or switches powered by a tiny atomic motor, from which could be projected the actual three-dimensional replica of historical events, scenes which had occurred in the far past. Stories were acted out and could be projected so that they seemed to appear in the air before the seer as if they were actual solid material form. All of the wisdom and knowledge that had been gained was thus preserved and was accessible to all.

Many evil and ancient beliefs in magic derived from the legends of this time, were only the remnants of the great science of the Atlanteans and those who preceded it. So-called magic is only unknown science which has been lost and forgotten by modern man.

The cross was a great symbol in ancient Atlantis. It was considered as a symbol of the earthly Eden from which four rivers flowed. This Eden and rivers symbolically has reference to the four Divine principles or powers known and used by the

Atlanteans. All the natural powers exercised by the Atlanteans depended upon the use of the etheric forces which they called Mana because these were in great part, controlled by the mental powers. This force later became related to Manas the mind of the Hindu Yoga.

Mana, or etheric essence, is a tremendous force, all-pervading, which may be tapped to supply illimitable energy. All so-called miracles are accomplished by conscious or unconscious tapping of this energy. In this case a sympathetic attunement is made. This knowledge, degraded, was the basis of all ancient sympathetic magic. Because space was filled with this mysterious essence which is subdivided into an almost countless number of kinds, the study of the heavens was undertaken to find the key to its releasement. This was the true origin of astrology and astronomy. In ancient times the astrologer could use a heaven chart as a means of tapping the inexhaustible reservoir for, sympathetically, an individual born under a certain configuration of the heavens was attuned with definite divisions or kinds of this etheric energy, under the sympathetic vibration law. It was for this reason that the Atlanteans developed special guilds born under different signs for the control of the twelve major divisions of the etheric energy.

There was on Atlantis the Golden Race, the Black Race, the White Race, the Blue Race, the Green Race, and a Red Race. Many of the races of modern times are descended from the mixtures of the various races of Atlantis, which were scattered over the earth after the sinking of the Motherland. Many of the colonies remaining were small in number, surrounded by barbarous races of tremendous strength and eventually were absorbed into those barbarous races, but in being absorbed, left their imprint in the color, the skin, some racial configurations, and in some, knowledge that they were able to impart even to the savage races.

The temple was sealed that still exists, buried through the silent ages at the bottom of the ocean. But in time to come Atlantis will rise again.

The Great Temple will be unfolded to the world with all of its mighty wisdom and secrets, but this will not occur until the Golden Age of man has dawned again. Man arising from his bondage to the beast will have taken his true place amongst the stars. At that time the Christ Kingdom will be established upon the earth. In the monumental remains great cities of the past, such as Tiahuanaco, in South America, and in great structures on the Caroline Islands we see the traces of a vast knowledge that man once had. When we read in Irish Mythology of the Tuatha De Daanan, the great people of Ancient Ireland, we are reading of the Atlantean colonies which existed in Ireland until a period of some 5,000 years ago. Men who had powers to fly through the air, travel under the water, disintegrate the atom and do many things that are unknown to our present science. But the Great Ones have passed and the knowledge that they once had, comes to us only faintly through legend and folklore of all of the races of the earth, because Atlantis left its imprint on all of the races and all of the religions of the ancient world. It is for that reason that the legend of Adam, the man of the red earth, is found amongst all the races of people of every part of the world.

It is for that reason that certain Universal symbols such as a cross, or the swastika, have been found in every land on every large island, even in the most remote places of the earth, because there was no spot so remote that the Atlanteans did not penetrate with their wisdom. There were no races so savage that some knowledge was not retained by them and the things that they had been taught by those of their ancient people who had been instructed on the Island of Undal.

MAP OF ISLANDS OF ATLANTIS

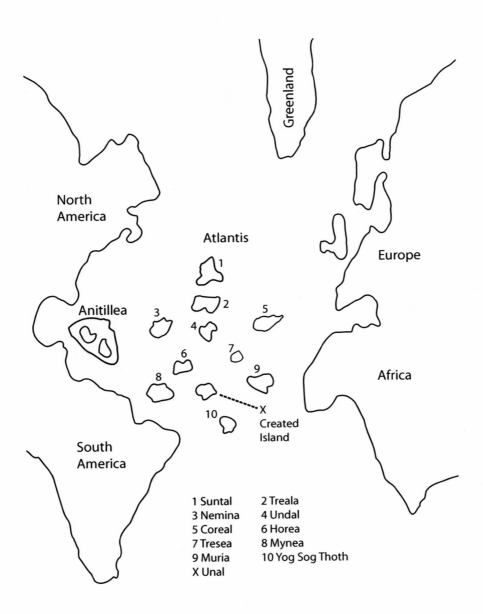

1 Suntal   2 Treala
3 Nemina   4 Undal
5 Coreal   6 Horea
7 Tresea   8 Mynea
9 Muria   10 Yog Sog Thoth
X Unal

ATLANTIS AND LEMURIA

BY DR. DOREAL

In legend it is said that there once existed in the Atlantic Ocean a great race who lived on a continent or group of Islands which now have as the sole remaining part above water, the Azores Islands. That group of Islands were called Atlantis, from which name our Atlantic Ocean was derived. Modern historical records only go back some five thousand or six thousand years.

According to the chronology as given in the Bible the world was created only a little over five thousand years ago. I have read manuscripts which were written a lot earlier than that, and I am convinced that the world has existed for many, many more than five thousand years.

About the only record that we have of Atlantis is found in the dialogue of Timeus by Plato. In it he tells that his grandfather heard from the Chaldean Priests about the continent or group of Islands which once existed in the Atlantic Ocean, and that the ancient Egyptians were immigrants or colonists. He says that there was a circle of water and then a land circle; then another mass of water and land mass. He said that according to the legend of the ancient Egyptians the God of the Sea, who created Atlantis, had a place upon which he built a palace for a human woman whom he loved and that he surrounded this place by alternate circles of land and water and that on these different circles he placed people and that they were ruled by the sons of Neptune or Posiedon the Sea God and this human woman.

According to Plato's dialogue by Timeus, Atlantis was the home of all wisdom and culture, and we are even told that the gods of ancient Greek and Roman mythology were nothing more or less than Atlantean kings or rulers, such as Atlas—who was an Atlantean.

According to the Chaldeans Atlantis had been destroyed in a great cataclysm some ten thousand years before their time. Then again, if we examine the legends of the Mayas of South and Central America, we find among other names the people of Atlan, or children of Atlantis. We know also that they have many legends about the existence of a mother land from which their ancestors came. (It is true that one of the Catholic Bishops destroyed all of the written records of the Mayas that he could get his hands on.)

Atlantis existed, and was a great civilization. It was destroyed about fifty-two thousand years ago. The great deluge mentioned in the Bible was the result of the sinking of the Atlantean and Lemurian continents. There are indications in South America of the existence of a great civilization.

The Mayans today have a mathematical system which is far superior to that which is taught in our schools and colleges in America. Certain very fine calculations can be made from the Mayan mathematical system—better than from our system. They also had considerable knowledge of architecture.

Some people say they were not civilized because they did not use a wheel on carts, but used sledges instead. To the Mayans, a wheel symbolized a circle of light or infinity, and they would not use it for any material thing, believing it should not be desecrated. For that reason they lack certain of the mechanical instruments which we have. The Greek alphabet from Alpha to Omega is nothing more or less than a collection of Mayan words which are the Atlantean origin, and in which is told the destruction of Atlantis and Lemuria. I refer you to Robert Ripley for confirmation of that.

Our Christian Bible mentions the great deluge or flood as having occurred a comparatively short time ago, whereas the records of the Chaldeans, from whom the Jewish people and the Hebrews derive their knowledge of the flood, place the time at what would today be approximately fifty-two thousand years ago.

Our geologists tell us that there was a great shaking and subsidence of a great part of the earth's surface some fifty thousand years ago. In the Amazon valley of South America there are remnants of vast cities, and works of such a nature that only a great civilized race could have built them. It is recorded that in the Amazon valley through which the Amazon River now flows, there was once a vast inland sea, and with the great shaking of the earth the lands began to rise and the Andes mountains were pushed up and the inland sea drained into the ocean. Thousands of feet up the Andes mountains today there are still remnants of a vast civilization—they are of the hardest basalt and granite ever conceived of. One building still stands, and it is so eroded by time that every carving on it has entirely vanished. No archaeologist or scientist has ever attempted to explain that place, nor the origin of a great engineering work just outside of that ancient city, which is a canal large enough, wide enough and originally deep enough for one of our big battleships to pass through. It is pushed up and goes over the mountains, and every few hundred feet it is broken and then goes on and up again. It was built before the Andes mountains were raised above the level plane and when the mountains were pushed up, this canal was pushed up with them. It is there today and can still be seen.

We also know that in 1872 when they opened up a mine there, they dug into the center of a hill and found a strange ship about one hundred and twenty feet long. It had no sail, but it had a peculiar metal apparatus on it with strange lenses. When the air struck it, it fell into dust. I have in my notes a record of the exact date upon which it was found. That ship had been there perhaps a hundred thousand years.

In Tibet, I have seen star maps which were up to five million years old. Man has been on this earth for a long, long time. Civilizations have risen and fallen. The North and South Poles were once tropical countries. When we think of the antiquity of man and of the comparatively   little that is know in modern times about ancient man, we sometimes wonder if man, as he is today, is the degenerated descendant of the great man, or is he, man, going upward again. We might say, "yes", and "no" on that.

Atlantis existed and sank fifty-two thousand years ago. At that time the world was in a very barbarous state; with the exception of the few colonies which were left by the Atlanteans very little culture and civilization existed because the continent of Lemuria had been almost destroyed some five hundred years before the sinking of Atlantis. There were numerous barbarous tribes in Africa, Asia and in parts of North America. There were also certain great Atlantean colonies in certain parts of the world. One was in Ireland. They have stories of the Tuatha Da Daanan having strange powers, now lost to man, who lived there once and ruled man. They had power to change their shape and take any form they wished to. If anyone displeased them they could play a tune on a pipe and the person would disintegrate. We are told that there came a time when they left there (Ireland) and went to some strange place of which they would not speak. But it was said that the time would come again when they would return.

The Chaldeans had a perfect record that they had been civilized and had originated from an Atlantean colony. There is another Atlantean colony recorded in California beneath Mt. Shasta—which is an extinct volcano. Mt. Shasta was not a Lemurian colony. Atlantis existed for over five hundred thousand years. During that time it was at the heighth of civilization and knowledge. They were developed and advanced in spiritual wisdom and unfoldment. Atlantis was a group of ten islands ruled by ten kings, which later, in legend, became ten circles alternately of land and water. The Azores in the Atlantic Ocean are a mountain peak of one of the ancient Atlantean Islands.

The Atlanteans had developed to great heights of civilization. They had learned all there was to know about the laws of nature, and they had become so civilized that there was established an absolute and perfect brotherhood amongst them. There was no poverty—they had everything that would make for absolute perfect material happiness. They had ten Islands and ten rulers, and they had a ruler of all of these Islands. They had a philosophical caste and a scientific caste, but they learned that the use of material laws was only a stepping stone to the knowledge of greater and higher laws. Finally they became such a great spiritual race, that the Great Ones among them began to pass closer to the spiritual Sun and their children were of a lower state of evolvement—they had great scientific powers and other vast powers at their beck and call but they did not have the spiritual power to use them rightly, and it was when that happened that Atlantis was destroyed, because the people had begun to misuse the things which they had. It was destroyed so that the knowledge which they had could be removed from man, and when man incarnated again it was in more barbarous races and he had to begin again to climb the long ladder of life.

Now I will speak of Lemuria. It was closely associated with Atlantis. (Books to read:—Atlantis-Antediluvian by Donnelly—History of Atlantis, by Lewis Spence.) From Norway every year there is a certain little rodent called "lemur" which leaves the land and begins to swim out into the ocean. It swims far out and then goes round and round in a circle and is finally drowned. It is an instinct in the animal to migrate to a land which must have once existed. Lemuria was in the Pacific Ocean; its coastline lay off what is now the Malay Peninsula, and the only extant parts of its land mass that are above the surface of the earth are the Caroline Islands in the South Pacific and close to no large land masses except the Malay Peninsula. They belong today to Japan. Before the World War they belonged to Germany. For the last twenty-five years no Americans were allowed to go there. The Japanese in working there found buried one hundred thousand coffins in pure platinum, and they are using this platinum to finance their war. They are called the Nan Matal and are composed of twelve Islands forming an almost perfect rectangle. Every one is based solidly around with basalt, with walls that rise forty feet high, and some of the stones in the wall weigh as much as thirty and forty tons. The stones are fitted together with no mortar, and yet are so solidly constructed that no sea water can get through. In some places there are steps leading up. Inside of the walls are the remnants of ancient temples. The Nan Matal and the surrounding Islands are solidly covered with great buildings built of giant stones, in some of which are still some carvings. These buildings are so enormous that it has been estimated by competent archaeologists that the population of the area must have been somewhere between four and one half and five million people. In other words, a city almost as large as London, in an area of two thousand square miles, where today there are less than fifty thousand people, and today there is not enough land and food products raised in an area of two thousand square miles to feed even a small part of the vast population which once must have inhabited that city.

The Polynesians say that beneath one of these Islands the Sun God is sleeping, and that some day he will awaken again and rule the world as he did once before. It is said that the entrance to this underworld is found in the Temple of the Sun God. At certain times of the month when the moon is full no Polynesian will approach for during that time it is said that there comes up from below a sound of voices chanting, and there is a certain ritual, and if a person is on the island at that time he is taken and never seen again. A number of white men have evidenced that there is such a sound coming up from below. The four who have been known to stay during the full of the moon did not stay there the whole three nights. These

Caroline Islands were known to the Ancients as the mountain peaks of Lemuria, and on the mountain the great temples and city are built. You can see the mountain down as far as you can look into the water, and divers have found buildings one hundred and fifty feet down. It is said that it was once a city of more than forty million people.

We are told that it was from this particular place that the moon was born. The moon is a child of the earth. Before the earth became solidified, as it was whirling around in space it cast off a part of itself which became the moon. Many scientists believe that when that happened it left a scar—a hollow space beneath, and this is the basis of the legends of the underworld with eight entrances, and that there will come from there, the Maitreya, King of the World who will rule the world.

When Lemuria existed above the surface of the world it was a vast and wonderful country and it had developed so far in scientific knowledge that it disturbed the Atlanteans who had turned toward the spiritual,—the Lemurians never had— they were a material nation. The Lemurians went further afield and established more colonies, and as a result they had considerable trouble with the Atlanteans because in a few places where the Atlanteans had settled, the Lemurians came and there was trouble. These two nations existed side by side—one a great spiritual nation, and the other a great material nation.

Atlanteans had turned, in their last days, towards spiritual development, and the Lemurians had become very physical. The Lemurians were the Hitlers of their day. They worshipped the snake god.

Before man came to Atlantis and Lemuria, these lands had been inhabited by a race which was not human. It was a strange race that had the body of a man but the head of a great serpent or snake. These beings were a hybrid manifestation and they had hypnotic power and could cause the head to assume the form or even the features of any person they desired. These snake people were almost totally destroyed by the Atlanteans and the Lemurians, but finally through centuries and thousands of years they began to appear again among the Lemurians and there they established the worship of the snake and serpent. Through their power they began to invade Atlantis and they caused their serpent head to assume the form of Atlantean leaders, and it got so, that the wise men of Atlantis searched out and discovered a word which the snake people could not pronounce, and every six months the rulers of the people were called before the people and told to pronounce the word which only human lips could pronounce, and thus the serpent worshippers would be revealed in their true light. The hypnotic, illusionary power of the snake people is responsible for the legends which we now have of the little snake being able to hypnotize things.

We are also told of a Great Temple on the islands of Atlantis which was ruled by one great person or entity, who in those times was called the Lord of Lords, and that he had existed since before the beginning of Atlantis. He was alive when Atlantis had its beginning and he was alive when Atlantis sank. He had manifested there for over five hundred thousand years, and he had power over all Atlantis, and it was he who led the Atlanteans onward and upward into a great spiritual nation. When Atlantis passed he went elsewhere, as did many of the great race. In my book (the Emerald Tablets) there is a translation of the life of a Great One who left Atlantis when it sank and migrated to Egypt and founded the Egyptian race. This is Thoth—the builder of the Great Pyramid.

Another thing about Lemuria—in Hawaii and among the Philippines we have some record in the ancient writings of the Lemurian race who left tablets and images on Easter Island that were built by the Lemurians. The great power and mastery which the Atlanteans had of the laws beyond and above the material laws caused Lemuria to sink—but that deluge was not the great deluge. The Great Deluge was the sinking of Atlantis itself. When Lemuria sank the ruling caste and the snake priests fled into a space which they had prepared for themselves for tens of thousands of years. It was that place from which the moon had been cast forth. The Lemurians had lived under the ground as much as they had lived over it. After the Lemurians had fled to that place, the Atlanteans sealed the entrance and placed a guard over it. That entrance is at the Sun Temple in the Caroline Islands. There is a story that from the top of Mt. Shasta, periodically, there is a great silver ship which flies over the Pacific. That ship goes to Nan Matal to inspect the seal where the Lemurians are imprisoned; those souls who have not passed beyond the bondage of the wheel of life go to that place between incarnations and work to help bring the Lemurians to a state of spiritual consciousness to free them from their imprisonment. The earth's surface has been changed four times in the past. Oklahoma and Texas were once a part of the ocean. Mexico has been up and down three times.

AN INTERPRETATION
OF THE
EMERALD TABLETS
BY DOREAL
WITH
THE TWO TABLETS
NOT PRINTED PREVIOUSLY

INTRODUCTION

In the following pages I will reveal some of the mysteries, which as yet have only been touched upon lightly, either by myself or other teachers or students of truth.

Man's search for understanding of the laws which regulate his life has been unending, yet always just beyond the veil which shields the higher planes from material man's vision the truth has existed, ready to be assimilated by those who enlarge their vision by turning inward, not outward, in their search.

In the silence of the material senses lies the key to the unveiling of wisdom. He who talks does not know; he who knows does not talk. The highest knowledge is unutterable, for it exists as an entity in planes which transcend all material words or symbols.

All symbols are but keys to doors leading to truths, and many times the door is not opened because the key seems so great that the things which are beyond it is not visible. If we can understand that all keys, all material symbols are manifestations, are but extensions of a great law and truth, we will begin to develop the vision which will enable us to penetrate beyond the veil.

All things in all universes move according to law, and the law which regulates the movement of the planets is no more immutable than the law which regulates the material expressions of man.

One of the greatest of all Cosmic Laws is that which is responsible for the formation of man as a material being. The great aim of the mystery schools of all ages has been to reveal the workings of the law which connect man the material, and man the spiritual. The connecting link between the material man and the spiritual man is the intellectual man, for the mind partakes of both the material and immaterial qualities. The aspirant for higher knowledge must develop the intellectual side of his nature and so strengthen his will that he is able to concentrate all the powers of his being on and in the plane he desires.

The great search for light, life and love only begins on the material plane, carried to its ultimate its final goal is complete oneness with the universal consciousness. The foundation in the material is the first step then comes the higher goal of spiritual attainment.

In the following pages I will give an interpretation of THE EMERALD TABLETS and their secret, hidden and esoteric meaning. Concealed in the words of Thoth are many meanings that do not appear on the surface. Light of knowledge brought to bear upon the Tablets will open many new fields for thought. Read and be wise, but only if the light of your own consciousness awakens the deep-seated understanding which is an inherent quality of the soul.

In the Threefold Light,
Doreal

TABLET I

The passing of Thoth into the Halls of Amenti was not the change we call death, he merely placed his physical body beneath the ray of force, later referred to as the cold Flower of Life, where it would be preserved indefinitely. As Thoth he would not return, but while his body rested in suspended animation his consciousness entered many bodies and lived many lives.

Keor was the city of the Priesthood of Atlantis. On Undal, the island just opposite Unal, there were two cities or rather two divisions of one great city that covered the island. The island was entirely surrounded by terraced walls and divided across the center by a high wall. Keor faced Unal and was occupied by the priesthood, while the other side of the island was known as CHIEN, and was occupied by the philosophic and scientific groups. No one was allowed on either part of the island excepting by a pass signed by the leaders of a group.

The mighty ones referred to were the adepts of Atlantis and these were thirteen in number. Thotmes, Father of Thoth, was head or chief of the thirteen. They operated on the principle of what later became the Great White Lodge. They knew the way to the Halls of Amenti, where for a time they would lie beneath the Flower of Life and rejuvenate their bodies. Unlike the masters they did not leave their bodies there while they incarnated in other bodies, but only bathed in the Fire of Life and renewed their bodies.

Thoth himself had descended to Amenti a thousand times to renew his body, and as this was necessary about once every fifty years, Thoth was approximately 50,000 years old at the time of writing. He was 20,000 years old at the time of the sinking of Atlantis, therefore, the writing of the Tablets must have occurred about 20,000 years ago.

Thoth lay his original body beneath the Flower of Light to be taken up again when he desires and sends his consciousness into other bodies through birth. He also says definitely that he will rise again in the flesh in a time yet to come. This time mentioned is spoken of later in The Tablets when the invaders from outer space attack the earth. The secrets which he left were the great ship of war beneath the Sphinx and the secret of the Pyramids. The men of Khem or Egypt, who were left as guards, have faithfully fulfilled the command and still guard the secrets. The Arcane Wisdom he gave them has enabled them to protect the secrets from the people who came after.

The people of Thoth were not the mass of Atlanteans, but the group which lived on Undal and comprised the scientific, philosophic and priest-classes. They had learned to seek knowledge at its source, the Akashic Records. The Children of Light came among them at times and taught them wisdom which enabled them to take the next step forward. The power of the eternal fire was the fire of the Universal Consciousness.

Thotmes, father of Thoth, was high-priest of Undal,

the mouth-piece of the Children of Light and the Dweller on Unal, to the kings and people of the islands.

Thoth was taught the mysteries which had been retained in the secret archives of the Temple. He had developed in the past to such a degree that he readily grasped the truths which were taught him. The desire for ultimate knowledge aroused such tremendous forces and placed him on such a plane of vibration that the Dweller became conscious of him.

The Dweller did not have the form or shape that man now has, but occupied a body similar to the bodies occupied by consciousness during the earliest part of the first cycle, the globular body. The light and force emitted by such a body was too great for the average human to stand. Only a consciousness on a high plane of vibration could stand it and still remain material.

The Dweller could see in Thoth one who was ready to have the Spark of Light fanned into flame. The arousing of the flame brought to Thoth life, stronger than the life of ordinary men, for as he grew in knowledge he was shown the path to the Halls of Amenti, where the Flower of Life force of this planet is concentrated.

Standing before the Lords of Life and Death he received the key of life and death, with power to take up life or lay it down, at will.

With the attaining of power over life and death Thoth was able to lay down his body and at will travel to the fartherest extensions of this space-time.

After tasting of the wisdom of the Cosmos he found

that it was centered in the hearts or minds of men. There he found greater mysteries, for it is through man that the Cosmos extends into unexplored territory.

Thoth was born about 20,000 years before the sinking of Atlantis, but because he had accepted a particular work he did not pass on as others did who had gained the first Illumination. Those who had been around him in youth passed on to Venus to be replaced by a wave of consciousness from Mars.

The later wave of consciousness was such that they could not be trusted with the science and wisdom of the earlier Atlanteans for they would have misused it. The Dweller spoke the Word of Power which was heard by the Lords of the Cycles dwelling in Amenti and they, hearing, directed the balance of the earth into new channels causing the land to sink, carrying with it the science and knowledge which the mass of people had. This knowledge, though nothing in comparison to the knowledge of the Children of Light, was yet too great to remain in the hands of undeveloped ones. The Flower of Fire is not in the Flower of the Fire of Life, but the pyramid of cold fire which is the balance of the earth.

The Temple of Light was not the Temple of Unal, but the outer temple of the priesthood on Undal. The Temple on Unal was never referred to as a temple, but only as the gateway or place of the Dweller, knowing of what it was composed it was never thought of as being subject to destruction and was, therefore, not considered in the sinking. Only a few of the wise men of Undal were left living when the rest of the land sank.

The land of the hairy barbarians is the land now known as Egypt. Khem was the first seat of learning established by the Atlanteans. From there later they sent emissaries to other barbarious tribes in different parts of the earth's surface. This was the plan mentioned, to use Khem as the central home of the new race-wisdom.

The ship of the master was a ship capable of traveling between planets and was armed with weapons that could destroy every living thing on earth's surface if used at full power. In the atmosphere it was driven by atomic motors, but outside the heavy side layer, it could be moved by thought, not only between planets, but into any space the mind of the pilot could visualize. Its structure was such that its materiality raised or lowered in vibrations as the will of the operator commanded.

As Thoth left the island of Unal, for, though he does not mention it, Undal had already gone down, the great Temple or place of the Dweller also sank, but was not destroyed.

The barbarians upon meeting Thoth and his followers, the Atlanteans, attempted to kill them, but were struck motionless by a paralyzing ray from Thoth's staff or rod of power. This rod was capable of transmitting or casting forth hundreds of different manifestations of force directed by the will of the holder.

The apparent supernatural power of Thoth caused the barbarians to submit to him and his statement to them that he was a child of the Sun is the basis for the worship of the sun among many ancient races. Thoth was, of course, referring to the Spiritual Sun.

It took many years to establish the new seat of the Children of the Sun, but when this was completed emissaries were sent to other races to teach and guide them.

As time passed Thoth found it necessary to open a passage to Amenti for the renewal of his body, for even though filled with power, after hundreds of years it began to disintegrate. This was necessary because his work was not yet finished.

After a long period of time the barbarians of Khem developed in consciousness until they could go forward without the aid of Thoth. Thoth plans to enter the Halls of Amenti and place his body under the Flower of Life while his consciousness goes elsewhere. The entrance to Amenti is below the Great Pyramid of Cheops of Khufu, builded by changing the atomic structure of stone until it became very light and then after it was in place changing it again. Beneath the Pyramid is the force-room connected with the apex of the Pyramid by a central shaft or well. In the upper portions of the shaft is a lens or crystal through which rays from the force chamber are directed. These are bent into time-space and curving open a dimensional pathway from beneath the Pyramid to the Hall of Amenti, which though in concurrent movement and space with the earth, exists in its own space.

The hidden chambers are the ones spoken of in the Book on the Great Pyramid. The Sarcophagus connects with the central shaft, and when one lies in it a specified length of time his body is transported down the shaft to the central force-chamber. The knowledge of this was preserved in later years, but debased into a ritual of initiation. It was first necessary to coat the body with a certain ointment for the occupant to be transported and the knowledge of this was not retained by the later Egyptians.

The Great Pyramid is indestructible, if its inner parts were disturbed forces would be let loose by the Guardians which would destroy anyone or thing which came against it.

Thoth later incarnated as Hermes and as other great teachers, though not always on earth.

Thoth leaves with the statement that those to come after will, in time, be able to tread the same path.

TABLET II

The Halls of Amenti are peculiar among hidden spaces of the earth, in that they are not in this octave of material vibration, but are in a fold of space set aside from all other spaces. They have a direct connection with the positive and negative polarities of the Yarkima and are thus flooded with light from not only the Cosmic Consciousness, but from the I. Yod. Their approximate location in relationship to the earth is beneath Atlantis, but one has to move out of this space fold to enter. There are various places where this can be accomplished: Sulphur Springs, Oklahoma; Mt. Shasta, California; Mictolan, South America; Shamballa, Tibet; Great Pyramid, Egypt; Black Forest, Germany; Benares, India; Atlas Mountains, Africa; Gobi Desert and an unnamed valley in Alaska. The far past time is the first cycle, which is fixed in past space-time, and is that particular period just after the negative descended on man and bound him in the material plane.

The Masters of that period or Children of Light formed their own bodies from the primal matter and imbued it with life. Though these bodies had the same outward form as man their interior structure was different, having sense organs usable only by a double unit of consciousness, male and female. They were not bound in the negative or disorder of man and were therefore free to accomplish things the rest of mankind could not accomplish. Whereas the physical body of Thoth had to be renewed every fifty years, the primal body required renewing only once in a hundred years.

It was in the first cycle that the Halls of Amenti were builded by the Children of Light who descended to this planet. By the forces they controlled they warped space and constructed Amenti and bound it to earth. The dimensional walls around it protected it from entry by any except the highest consciousness. The great space was sub-divided into other smaller spaces and direct concentrations of force from the Yarkima were centered in them.

There were thirty-two of these Children of Light on the earth, having charge of the affairs of earth.

In the Halls was placed a concentration point of vital life force or spirit. Into it is poured that vital force of life which supplies the very life of the planet. When an object on earth disintegrates the spirit which is freed, is drawn to the Flower of Life in Amenti to be called forth at need. It acts for earth in the same capacity as the solar-plexus acts for the human body.

The thrones of the Children of Light were so placed that they were in the full flow of spirit which supplied their bodies as fast as they lost their own flow. Thus a body placed under it did not have to draw life directly from the source, but bathed in its radiance the balance was fully maintained when the consciousness was away, even though it be for centuries.

The life force is so strong that the reservoir of the body, placed under it for a hundred years, was so filled that it would last a thousand years without renewal. Thus, ten years of each hundred would keep the body young and powerful.

In most instances the body was left for great periods of time and the Children of Light entered the bodies of men through birth, but occasionally they came forth in their original bodies, though not often.

When one has attained the third Illumination he is made free of Amenti and can, if he desires, place his body beneath the Fire of Life and renew it from age to age.

The Seven Lords are direct emanations or extensions from the Seven Cosmic Consciousnesses beyond this. They work independent of, and yet in harmony with this cosmic consciousness. They have control of certain forces from beyond such as negative disorder and have emanations on all inhabited planets in this Cosmos. Other functions of the Lords are the control of time-space, separating the four times and the holding back of an onrush of disorder from the negative reservoir upon the flames of consciousness which have broken away from it. It is their power which draws life force into its concentration point in the Flower of Life and holds it there.

The Lord of Lords is the emanation from the ninth Cosmic Cycle and holds his or its title because it is the most highly developed and fartherest extension of this I. Yod. It is the power which controls the negative in all Cosmic Cycles. Below him, but equal in regard to purpose and control of their own particular powers are the Lords of the other six cycles above us. Though not of this cosmic consciousness they are akin to it for all are formed forth from the same basic material, ordered disorder and have been born from the same source, the I. Yod, the Primal Source of Creation.

Thoth was brought before the Lords by Horlet, the Dweller on Unal, and there watched the Dweller blend with one of the Lords, in other words enter into such harmony that they become one. From him came forth a voice, the Lords not being of human form or vibration could not speak in words, their power was stepped down so that Thoth could hear. Later he became able to raise his own vibration so that he could hear the silent voice of the Lords, but this did not occur until he had passed certain tests.

Thoth was given freedom of Amenti or was given the key whereby that space could be opened by him at will, and having access to the Flower of Life need die only when he willed.

Thoth learns the laws of creation so that he can take up any form or body he desires. Following the law he must now choose what particular work he will do, for attainment of illumination brings greater opportunity and power to work. The height to which Thoth has attained is only a foothill of the greater mountains of transcendental light toward which all cosmic consciousnesses are working. As Thoth had attained one goal he could henceforth walk with those seeking a greater goal.

It was one of the thirty-two Children of Light, not one of the Lords who conducted Thoth on his first tour of the

Halls of Amenti. The Halls of Amenti, the places wherein the antithesis of life (which is death) reigned. This force being somewhat akin to that which is called life is found in the place of life. It may seem paradoxical to call death akin to life, but if we realize that it is through the action of death on the negative that life becomes freer we can see its kinship.

The Lord of Death is not one of the Lords from cycles above, but is of this cosmic cycle. He has charge of the action of death-force upon the negative which surrounds each spark of consciousness. That darkness, which is loss of consciousness or death, is called night, for in it the consciousness loses memory of that which has been. He is told not to touch Thoth with loss of consciousness.

The Lord of Death is told to see and recognize Thoth as a Sun of Light, not to be held or touched by death. The hand of the Lord of Death is raised, sending forth flame, symbolical of the Light concealed in the darkness of death. Light banishes the darkness and Thoth is shown uncounted millions of flames each a soul manifesting on this plane. The brightness or dimness of the flame showed the degree of negative disorder in which they were bound.

The Lord of Death tells Thoth of the mysteries of life and death, explaining how the soul incarnates in a physical body, reaches the zenith of its growth and then passes through change, to leap forth again with greater light.

Death comes, but only as a temporary thing; life itself is immortal, existing from the beginning to the end.

Always in the end life and light must conquer death and darkness. Death desires that light banish his power for even death came forth from light. Thoth is shown his own soul as it drives out the darkness and flames forth into full light. The Guide then leads Thoth into other great spaces in Amenti and elsewhere, showing him mysteries revealed only to adepts. Among others he was shown the inner spaces of the fourth dimension. Thoth was again brought before the Lords and by the Lords who had first spoken to him, was commanded to choose his work. Thoth, of his own accord, chooses to become a teacher, bringing souls from darkness into Light. He is verified in his choice by the Lord and commanded to go forth and work as he has chosen.

Thoth is led upward to earth, there fulfilling the choice he has made. He closes with the statement that now again he goes to Amenti, leaving man for a time.

TABLET III

The key of wisdom containing some of the precepts given by Thoth to the barbarians, the Children of Khem, was given so that the Keys of Light should not be lost to man.

Wisdom and power walk hand in hand, without both either is useless and non-existent, for power is not created without wisdom and wisdom is only attained through development and use of power.

The proud person is not wise but foolish, for pride causes the proud one to reject learning for he measures all things by his own rule and standards. Silence is golden, talking about evil turns the creative force upon it and gives it life and actuality.

To attempt to rise beyond the law brings its own punishment for nothing is beyond law and the one who attempts to operate against law breaks himself against law.

Fear should not be allowed to enter self, neither should we create fear in another, for fear is bondage. If within our hearts we have kindness then those of like harmony are attracted to us—if this is not the case then that one is ruled by disorder.

The commands of the master within are the ones to be followed and do not attempt to objectively do more. Riches are a means to an end, not the end—when the material needs are supplied the mind (the hearts of the ancients) should lead into higher realms.

It is necessary to have a guide while on the path, otherwise one is led astray by attempting to find an easier way.

Love is the beginning and end of the path for in love lies oneness. Thoth gave this especially to the tribes to inculcate the teachings of brotherhood and oneness.

The person who comes in trouble finds a relief in expressing himself. If he is hesitant it is because the one to whom he has come has some flaw in his own nature which repulses.

This statement is of great value. Extravagant speech always shows lack of balance and it is harmful to either speak in such manner or listen, for most people are easily thrown off balance. Perfection is the only goal, you should not be satisfied with anything short of it. It is only lack of knowledge which prevents one from penetrating the veil behind which lies wisdom.

Silence is the great key to advancement; retain power within thyself in silence. Make not yourself great for all have potentially the same power.

True greatness does not require self-praise, let others acknowledge your greatness which is recognized by your attitude toward your fellowman.

Each person finds a reflection of his own nature in the one before him, therefore, listen not to the things others may say about a person. Only by examining his mind and his attitude toward his fellow can you find his true nature.

If you store knowledge do not withhold from one in need who earnestly asks. All are friends who seek the same goal.

Do not let the words of an ignorant fool affect thee, only the ignorant are affected by the ignorant. The vibrations from the mind of a person are perceptible, words are not necessary.

Thoth again gives a discourse on the mysteries, giving keys and symbols for interpretation by those who are ready.

The immaterial part of man's nature, the soul, must be separated from man's material nature, the flesh before it can go into the light of the Cosmic Sun. The soul is the fire while the flesh is akin to earth. Each returns to its source. The inner fire penetrates to all planes in which the great fire manifests, including the material. Earth being dense supports within a limited range even the fire of the soul, otherwise the soul being infinite would change finite earth to an infinite thing.

It is the development of consciousness which allows the eye to see color and light. The infinite fire, developing and changing eternally also develops the perceptions.

Man is a changing fire, never the same, thus he ever advances from day to day until he rises above the darkness which does not change while it is still darkness. However, darkness becomes so infused with fire that it ceases to be darkness.

Strife, hatred and fear are the results of darkness,

freedom from darkness eliminates these. Name and form, otherwise individual separation, cease to exist in the full light of awakened consciousness.

The creative ability comes with the opening of the third eye and are the effects of the training required to fully open that eye.

Man attains only through effort and experience for such are the purifying agents which cleanse the dross of darkness from the soul.

Materiality is but an unconscious form of manifestation of consciousness, thus in the final analysis materiality and immateriality are one. Nothing that is material is fixed, it is constantly passing through change, this is its path from creation onward. Man adds a consciousness to this law of nature.

Law, in its final analysis is all that exists, all other things are phantasies and illusions formed in the minds of those without knowledge.

Wisdom comes only to those who seek her, you must take the first step and then continue to walk forward.

The Halls of Death beneath the Halls of the Flower of Life contained the reflection of the souls of men. It was there that Thoth could read the story of Man's advancement from darkness to light.

A seeming paradox is contained in the words brought from the future of infinity's end. The Torch Bearer of Insupportable Brightness is the beginning and the end of all things, for as all things proceeded forth from it, so in the end they must return to it, thus completing the circle. In the Torch Bearer the eventual is conceived, thus the plan is known to the direct emanation, the Lords.

The Seven is the title of the Lords of the Cycles beyond us, each called by the number of his cycle in its relationship to the I. Yod.

Coming from cycles beyond this they are part of the absolute essence of each of these cosmic consciousnesses. They are bound to neither life nor death, for their activity is controlled directly by the Yarkima. Thus their life is not the life of emanations from a cosmic cycle as they are not dependent on spirit for manifestation.

The Logos, meaning word or reason, is an emanation from the Lords of each cycle (always remember that there is a Lord of this cycle, also, not included in the seven) as it is literally an emanation of pure reason from the I. Yod. As this comes along the Yarkima and they are the central cell through which it flows.

They are vast in countenance for they extend into all cosmic spaces, yet are small because they are centered in form.

Three, the Lord of the Cycle just beyond us is the custodian of those things which directly affect mankind. He is responsible for the entrance of the negative and it is through his power that the reflections of the souls of men were focused in the Halls of the Dead.

The flow and direction of that force which we know as life force is controlled by the Lord of Four. Some of the greater forces such as death are drawn from Four, a cycle where life ceases to be, that is as we know life. The Lords each have their function, affording entrance into this Cosmic Space in powers which they have developed in their own progress through space. This is stepped down and transmitted through the Lords, each giving of what he has to those below.

The fifth is guardian of the Word, opening the final gate when man is ready for it. Six, Seven and Eight have charge of certain of the fixed skeletal frameworks of future time, while Nine takes charge of disorder after it becomes order. In a way they are assistants to this Cosmic Consciousness, carrying out aspects necessary to the development of consciousness that this Cosmic Consciousness is not as yet capable of handling.

In these numbers also lie a key to the Word, but as yet this cannot be given. Attainment of it is indeed the attainment of Life and Light.

TABLET IV

Thoth in this tablet gives some of his own experiences in his search for wisdom. He also gives a definite statement of his mastership.

The breaking of his soul from bondage was the first projection of his consciousness. Through this developed power Thoth was enabled to explore the mysteries of space and time. He explored other planets and ultimately reached the inner circle of light, the first dimension.

The planet of beauty was one of the seven inner planets which surround the cosmic consciousness in the first dimension. The shapes moving in order were the globular bodies of illuminated ones.

Thoth was able to go into all solar systems and see the different degrees of development reached on the planets closest and fartherest from the Sun. By men are designated those forms of life activated by conscious consciousness, though their forms were seldom that of earth-man.

The conquerors of ether were the dwellers on Antares, the same race that had come to earth in past ages. They had solved the secret of interplanetary travel ages ago, for they were the most enlightened ones of their solar system. Matter and form were theirs to command and from the Universal Mother they were able to create anything they desired.

Thoth learned that man was universal, existing in every part of space and an integral part of the cosmic consciousness. The form of man so far as its materiality was concerned was one with the basic matter of the stars. As planets revolve around their sun, so the material body of man revolves around its central sun, the soul. When one has freed his consciousness from the darkness of disorder he becomes one of those masters who work upon the negative from outside. Man's body is formed from the primal substance, cosmic dust, and the ether in which the planets float is also cosmic dust.

The solving of the mysteries of space gives the causes behind many manifestations of law which otherwise could not be understood.

Thoth now knew that endlessly he could explore the gem of truth until at last he might pass into the cosmic cycle beyond this. Thoth was free because he now knew that truth is limitless and now through eternity he could pursue knowledge.

Man is not truly of the earth or material, but in the final analysis, is the Divine fire itself.

Thoth gives the Key to the freedom of consciousness from the material and this freedom opens the path to other worlds and planes. When this is once attained man is no longer bound, but is free. Only through knowledge comes the ability to rise from the earthly body and become one with the light.

As space is ordered and follows law, so man must also cause order to arise within his own being. When this order and harmony of all parts of his being is perfect, then he no longer is bound to the material plane and rising through his harmony with law he can ascend to the Cosmic Plane.

In freeing the consciousness from the body it is best to expand the solar-plexus (the Flower of Life of the body) and send the life force flooding through it so that the body is vitalized in preparation for the consciousness to leave, otherwise the consciousness is reluctant to leave it. Then comes the shutting off of outside sensory impressions which should be preluded by a short fast.

After the silence induced by the will is complete the consciousness should be centered in the pineal and the image thought or picture of the place you desire to go should be formed; then an intense effort of will directed in the proper curves (See College Lessons of the Brotherhood), and you are released from the body.

The Cosmic Consciousness is literally speaking in the first dimension or plane and its harmonies and order are such that man, while still of the material, cannot realize its perfect movement.

The soul of man is a Divine fire, a flame cast forth from the great fire yet still one with it. Light in darkness is man, yet separate in power and order.

The prayer is really a command and is for the purpose of establishing a harmony or connection between the soul or consciousness and the cosmic consciousness.

When man has fully freed his soul from bondage to the material, then he is no longer subject to disorder or negative and can seek wisdom at the source of wisdom.

TABLET V

This perhaps is the most mystical of the Tablets, containing also information hitherto withheld from man. Thoth is musing on the glories of Atlantis at its zenith as compared to the world around him at that time.

The Dweller on Unal, the Master Horlet, was ruler of all the earth (through the Cosmic Power he wielded) though he did not intervene in the government of nations unless it was absolutely necessary.

Horlet was not entirely of this cycle, but was one of the extensions of one of the Lords of the Cycles, manifesting on earth's surface to fulfill certain necessary functions, helping to establish knowledge and harmony among men. He established the kingdoms of Atlantis, dividing them among the races and placing the highest developed ones as kings over the rest of men.

He then built the Temple on Unal from the ether or primal substance, molding it to form by his will, using the power of Ytolan (not translated) to hold it in form. The Temple was square and had three miles to a side and was a mile high. It did not truly rest in third dimensional space, but in the ninth dimension, therefore the blackness. No weapon from the third dimension could harm or even touch it for anything cast against it would be lost in the curves of the ninth dimension. It had within its heart the essence of light for there was the gateway to Amenti where the Flower of Life burns eternally.

The Dweller used the Word in molding the form of the Temple, the Word being then expressed as Ytolan. Within the Temple the Dweller erected mighty machines of many kinds, forming them out of primeval matter and started them in motion by his will, thus actuated they would run forever for the will which supplied their motive power is an eternal thing.

In the Temple the Dweller was at most times unmanifest, that is the physical body which he occupied from time to time remained in the Temple while the consciousness which was he, manifested elsewhere.

Three from among the highest developed of men were chosen to be messengers of the Dweller. These were carefully trained in their work by the Dweller while through them he chose others and had them placed on Undal, opposite Unal to be teachers and priests to Atlantis. These later were the priests, scientists and philosophers. Each of these was taught for fifteen years by the three before he was allowed to teach others.

Thoth made his first contact with the Dweller through one of the three messengers. He was led before the Dweller in the Temple in the place of the great fire. This fire was not the Fire of Life, but the radiation caused by the junction of the space of the Temple with the space of Amenti.

Thoth was led before the Dweller who, seated on the throne, reflected the light from the gateway. To Thoth he appeared to be literally clothed with fire. He was informed by the Dweller that he was chosen to be keeper of the records, for the Dweller could look into man's future, knowing the changes in consciousness would eventually bring a wave of units of consciousness of low development to earth. He also knew the destruction of parts of earth's surface must come, so steps must be taken so that nothing would be lost. Thoth had earned this great privilege by his own effort.

The reference to the Dweller as Master of Cycles is a reference to earth cycles not cosmic cycles. He was the guardian of Man's progress from one earth cycle to another. Thoth asks for wisdom to be given him so that he can pass the knowledge he is to be given to man.

Thoth is promised eternal life so that he may fulfill his purpose. He remained in the Temple until he received his full illumination.

Thoth uses the knowledge given him to penetrate the secrets of space, time and matter and in these discovers ever more and greater secrets.

In the latter days of Atlantis the great wave of consciousness which had once occupied the bodies of earth men had passed to Venus and the consciousness which occupied the bodies of the mass were from Mars. These were more materialistic than the preceding consciousness and looking to the darkness instead of the light opened Yog-Sog-Thoth, the gateway to the cycle below. Some of the consciousnesses of the preceding wave were attracted by material power and entered into the plans. It was perhaps this part of their nature which had kept them from going on with their fellows. The one who opens the door to the cycle below must be a master else he will not be so balanced in power that he can keep those from below from coming up. While men were doing this the Dweller was detached from his body and projected to where it was taking place.

When the Dweller saw what was taking place he returned to his body and called the messengers and sent them through Atlantis, bringing certain ones to Undal. The Dweller then descended to Amenti and passed from there to force chambers opening into the channel through which earth's balance passes (See "Inner Earth"). When the Pyramid of force passed he drew upon the power of the seven and changed the balance of earth from one channel to another and closed the old channel.

The resulting sinking of Atlantis shattered the opening by destroying the space-warping machines set up by the Atlanteans.

Thoth is called before the Dweller and commanded to go forth to the lands still above water, taking those from Undal and removing the records of the ancient wisdom. He is commissioned as teacher or conveyor of light.

Thoth gathered together the records, scientific instruments and machines and with the wise men of Atlantis entered a space ship and flew to Khem.

The motive power of the space ship was energy extracted from the sun and stored. Electricity is one form of this force but qualified by emanations from the pyramid of force.

When the space ship had left, the Dweller sealed the Temple and sank it and Undal beneath the waves. He and the three then went elsewhere.

Thoth arrived in Egypt and conquered the barbarians. He then buried the space ship and certain implements of warfare beneath a great rock which was then carved as the Sphinx. When the time arrives that invaders from space attack the earth it will be brought forth to repel them.

Thoth gives a key for opening the hidden passage from the Pyramid to the Sphinx. The same key will open the doorway to the room from which opens the path to Amenti.

TABLET VI

In this Tablet Thoth speaks of magic, using the term to denote the usage of developed power in the warfare between forces of order and disorder. This warfare has continued since the fall of man in the first cycle and will continue until the cosmic consciousness is ready to pass through Suntal.

There are adepts who use the great powers of the Cosmos for destruction instead of construction for law operates either for good or evil, positive or negative. Those adepts who used cosmic force for destruction were the dark brothers, black magicians who fought against the Children of Light. They attempted to hold and pull back those whom the Children of Light were trying to bring into Light.

The Black Brotherhood is the antithesis of the White Brotherhood, one destroys, the other builds. The Black Brotherhood has an organization known today as the Black Dugpas, the adepts having their chelas as the White Adepts have. They pattern their organization after that of the White Lodge and oft times deceive men into thinking they are of the White Lodge. They help men to gain certain things and powers until they have them in their toils, then when there is no escape they clamp down. They have certain specific powers developed such as opening the seventh dimension and calling in elementals to fulfill their purposes. They have the power of mind control through thought transference and hypnosis. Through this they gain control of the mind and lead it into disorder. If one surrenders to the Black Brotherhood and signs his name in their book he is bound to them during that incarnation.

Man's soul must not be bound if it desires to advance in light, surrender to the dark forces entails the shutting off of light. Only through darkness and disorder is man bound to the flesh, therefore, he should become light and ordered.

The Black Brotherhood always tries to pull down the person who has gained development along the path of light, for they have already developed powers. It is for this reason that the person who is highly developed has to withstand more than the person of little or no development. The more one has learned of light, paradoxically, the more he knows about manipulation of disorder and the more valuable he is to the Black Brotherhood.

The development of reason and balance is necessary so that we can separate darkness from light, order from disorder in the words of those who come to us. Only through overcoming obstacles and continual striving will the goal be attained.

In opposition to the Black Brotherhood stand the White Lodge striving constantly to free men from disorder and warding off the powers of the Black Brotherhood. If the seeker has his real desire on light, not power, the White Lodge will stand between him and the Black Brotherhood for they have greater power than the Black Brotherhood, yet the Blacks are allowed to exist for they form part of the darkness which man must overcome, and rise above.

The warfare between the forces of the Black Brotherhood and the White Lodge, has continued since the beginning.

The Masters and Great Adepts of the White Lodge use the power of the awakened Sun in man to guard and protect. The Children of Light, they who never lost their original oneness, are also guardians of man who is their brother. They are custodians of secrets that push back the darkness and these are given to the ones who travel the way toward mastership.

The one who desires to be a master must learn mastery of the laws which regulate manifestation, he must conquer fear and walk unafraid on the pathway of Light.

The secrets of Thoth regarding the operation of the law of protection are offered. Only by knowing can you conquer.

You must use knowledge given, otherwise it is useless. Many of the vibrations which seem negative are really from within our own self, not from outside conditions. Lack of mind-balance often results in the arousing of such negative thoughts that we really feel as if outside entities or forces were at work on us. Apply the light of reason to the disturbance and find if it is from within or without. If from within start a vibration in the pineal and send it in irregular waves through the body, that is, send the first wave through, count one, send another wave, count three, another wave, then two and so on. After doing this for a while send it through in regular waves in this manner. Send wave, count two, wave, two and so on.

If upon examination you find that it is an outside force you should go into a dark room or cave and draw a circle around yourself, not closing the circle until you are within it and follow the formula as given.

The formula given is serviceable for others as well as yourself. The power given may be used.

TABLET VII

This Tablet opens with a command to open your mind to the wisdom of Thoth. He says that life is filled with obstacles that must be conquered. The light of the Cosmic must be allowed to flow into and through the manifestation. The goal of all seeking must be oneness with the cosmic consciousness, otherwise there is limitation.

Light is both finite and infinite, because God, the Cosmic Consciousness, is light and all things manifest and unmanifest are a part of God, therefore, there can be no real separation. Even in the veil of darkness, which we call negative, the essence of light is hidden ready to spring forth when the veil is sundered.

The infinite brain is lost to the comprehension of men who do not realize that everything is only separate manifestations of the one cosmic brain.

All aspects of wisdom either in Gods or men are parts of the one wisdom manifesting through diversified channels.

Law and order are the fundamental rules of all creation, either in God or man, for only in order is balance or equilibrium found.

Thoth is again speaking of the far past time before Atlantis sank. His first introduction was through the Dweller, but afterward he knew the key and was able to enter himself. How different he was from most seekers today, when given a key he used it.

The Lords of the Cycles taught Thoth of the cycles beyond so that he had a knowledge of them and their workings even though he could not penetrate through Suntal to the higher cycles.

Thoth promises to give of the wisdom he had learned.

We are told that the Lords are guides to man and this they are for they teach him of those things which are beyond the scope of this cosmic consciousness and he thereby gains knowledge of the extensions of the I. Yod.

According to the ancient symbolism, wisdom was found in the flame. Fire coming from the unmanifest, existing for a time in the manifest and then disappearing into the unmanifest became the symbol for consciousness, which comes from the unmanifest, exists for a time in the physical body and disappears back into the unmanifest. Thus man is literally told to seek wisdom within his consciousness.

The seven had come from beyond cycle time which is limited, depending as it does upon radiation from the original infinite atom. The Seven were part of the cosmic consciousness which came forth from the I. Yod before we did and were therefore formed while we were still part of disorder.

They had developed past the man stage, though when they occupied this cosmic cycle they were like men. Consciousness in the ultimate is formless and flexible, assuming any form of which it has conception.

Thoth is told that now he is free to travel the path until the final circle is completed and that which was once one, again becomes one.

The cosmic consciousnesses which occupy the cosmic cycles beyond us were formed in ordered sequence, not all at once. There are seven of these beyond us, that is farther out in space from the I. Yod.

These Lords though manifesting here are still connected with their own cosmic consciousness.

Infinity is but a part of the greater space which we call transcendental. When the I. Yods have completed their extension into infinite space they will join the Torch Bearer in transcendental space.

The spirals of time-space must be consciously known to one before he can move in them. When space and time are known one has developed the power to move backward and forward in space and time. Life and Death exist only as comparative terms, everything has its opposite, remove one pole and the other ceases to exist. In the plane of consciousness in which the higher cosmic consciousness of nine manifests, death is not known, therefore, life also in not known. There is only existence, immortal and eternal without change of focal point of manifestation or loss of conscious consciousness.

When man conquers death he also has mastered life and to him both cease to exist. The Lord of nine in his own plane is timeless for time is a result of the existence of materiality and the ninth cosmic consciousness does not manifest a materiality.

The soul of man is the flame which is bound to the mountain, flesh. When we have become one with the I. Yod in the final completion of the infinite circle, materiality and life which is one with death will cease to exist.

In the eighth cycle also, life and death are one and only eternal existence manifests. The eighth cosmic cycle is the cycle of light, for here the infinite light is concentrated upon the disorder sent from the ninth cycle, breaking it into divisions of kind which are transmitted to lower cosmic cycles as disorder changed to order is the basis of everything, light is master of all that exists.

When the two parts of a unit of consciousness have become fully one and the other parts have become one with the one, thus becoming all, it is not impossible to go forward into the higher cosmic cycle.

Thoth states clearly that all parts of his unit are one when he says that his goal is the all-thing. Thoth uses a prayer to light, but as always ends with a command.

To the light, what we call form is formless, for only in the light does true reality exist. Thoth gives freely of his wisdom so that others may tread the same path.

He commands his followers to ever keep their faces toward the light, turning their thoughts toward the master within, thus shall they avoid the glittering promises of material power promised by the Dark Brothers.

TABLET VIII

Thoth had attained the power of mastership and with it the ability to enter any interlocking world and there take on form and also the ability to enter the inner spaces of the fourth dimension.

In symbols, the keys of wisdom are found, only those who search for the hidden meanings find the way. There is constant change and evolution in man, both as material and spiritual. As he develops in consciousness he blends more and more with the essence of consciousness which is formless in the ultimate, and finally he attains to that cosmic cycle wherein nothing material manifests in form.

Thoth commands them to search out the mysteries of the inner earth and learn of the balance of earth, the pyramid of force which is composed of the essence of that force which causes atoms to cast off particles of themselves. Man must find the pyramid and stand either in body or projection before it receiving its universal force.

He commands them to enter the blue lighted Temple which is the great Hall of Amenti, where the seven sit. Man is both body and consciousness, but the consciousness, the flame, must absorb the body—earth.

Only through striving can wisdom be found, hidden as it is within darkness, and yet in that darkness the essence of flame exists and in this is the true wisdom found.

The Kingdom of Shadows was that octave of vibration in which were placed those brought from a lower cosmic cycle when the gateway was opened by man. This was in the third or Polarian Cycle and the delvers in darkness were men who loved material power, rather than to devote their lives to spiritual things. The beings called up were formless, as only the consciousness was brought up and bodies must be formed here.

They, like the elementals, being separated from their own cosmic consciousness and its creative powers and were not able to combine with this cycle because they had not developed its primal curves. Only by the will of man and the extracting of spirit from blood could they take form.

The masters drove most of them back through the lower gateway but there were some who remained in the place built for them, coming forth only when the name was called and the blood sacrifice was offered. They took on the apparent form of man, but their actual appearance was the body of man or woman with a serpent head.

They were able to cast a hypnotic glamour around them and appear to assume the features of men. It is this which forms the basis for the belief in the hypnotic powers of the serpent. They assume the forms of leaders who were secretly slain and gradually they and the men who called them took over the control of the nations. They had all of the appearance of men, but there was one word they were unable to pronounce. This was taught by the masters to man and it became a law that every man who had office must pronounce this word before the people once each lunar month. If he failed he was killed. This forced them from place among men and gradually they were forgotten, but some still exist in their own place, unable to enter because man has forgotten the rites which summon them. The word was—KININIGEN.

The master of either white or black magic may summon them, but only a white master may have the power to control them. They rule through fear, conquer fear and you have gained light.

Thoth states that he has been to Suntal and even looked within the sixth dimension. They move only through angles and never through curves. The projected consciousness which tries to penetrate the sixth dimension will infallibly be attacked by the Hounds of the Barriers, only by moving through space in circles, can you evade the hounds. Only in the circle is protection, return to the body is of no avail. However, one does not stumble upon them accidentally.

Thoth had this experience in the past and it taught him caution. He attempted to pass the gateway, Suntal, and the guardians came at him. He knew the law of circles and angles and evaded them, returning to his body and completing the protection. The Hounds of the Barrier do not literally devour or destroy the soul, but bind it from further manifestation until this cosmic cycle is completed, then it may combine with the next cosmic consciousness. Even after completing his protection he must be careful not to approach the sixth dimension in angular movement.

Thoth repeats again and again his warning about movement through curves. He also tells them not to attempt to pass Suntal before the time, for few have succeeded. He also tells how to recognize the guardians.

TABLET IX

The first page consists of commands to seek the light rather than darkness so that you may realize the oneness of all things.

The command is given to seek for wisdom and not allow the material to hold you back for only wisdom creates harmony.

Even in the time in which Thoth wrote the wisdom of the ancient races was forgotten among the people who were descendants of the barbarian tribes Thoth found after he left Atlantis.

Man is part of the essence of consciousness but that knowledge is forgotten by the mass of mankind.

Thoth through projection of consciousness realized that consciousness is the ultimate reality and that the body was the fetter which binds man to the physical world. Through experience gained in projection he learned of the curves and angles of space.

Thoth begins to state some of the laws which were as mysterious to the mass of people of his time as they are today.

That which seems to be the totality of all things is only one facet, one aspect of the Jewel of Truth.

Matter is fluid insomuch as it is constantly disintegrating to be formed into new combinations. Other spaces spoken of are interlocking worlds, the inner spaces of the fourth dimension and the other dimensions.

The frequency of the number nine is spoken of including nine Lords of Cycles though we are told only of the seven. The nine include the Lords of this Cosmic Cycle and the one below.

Time-space is spoken of as being full of concealed ones; the concealment being behind the curves of the space-spiral. As consciousness in some form is present in everything it follows that it must also be in the diffusions of past-time matter.

In and through man alone can the path to other planes be opened.

The circle represents completion of the opening of the channel of force passing through the centers of the body. The Word is the vibration which loosens the power. Only through this can life really be realized.

Man is not material, though seeming to be. He is light, springing from the eternal source and only appearing as a material being and even materiality is only so in seeming, for in the ultimate the material becomes light.

Thoth seeks constantly for more wisdom to add to that which he already has.

Thoth journeys to the Halls of Amenti to ask the Lords the question; "Where is the source?" He is commanded by the Lord of Nine to free himself from the body, for only in the spirit can this be truly answered. Thoth frees himself from the body and is cast into the abyss, literally the great deep and is there shown the moulding of order from disorder. The Lord of Nine has temporarily harmonized him with the full flow of the Yarkima and he can see into the I. Yod, in the Arech and see the creation and forming of a Cosmic Consciousness.

We are shown that the true Word is Order, which changes all disorder into its own likeness. The life in man is a manifestation of order and therefore a key to the Word. If you can realize the full meaning of the passage you have the key to the Lost Word.

Life is an expression of the order which proceeds forth from the absolute fire of the Torch Bearer. We are thus again shown that the Word is order and harmony. The path to the Word lies in ordering your life so that chaos is eliminated from it. Man is lost from the Word because he has allowed disorder and chaos to rule his life. Every effort put forth, every conquest of disorder brings us closer to the Word.

TABLET X

The thought which grew in the abyss was the first expression of activity and movement. Without law, which is order, nothing could exist in form.

Time, the great secret is a key to freedom, for when man conquers time he has also conquered death.

The infinite jewel of truth can never be fully read for truth brings forth extensions of itself and as one truth is mastered other truths appear.

Thoth questions the Dweller about time and space and the Dweller tells him of the beginning of all things in the great void.

He tells him of thought which sprang into being and is questioned as to thought being eternal. The answer of the Dweller is so plain as to need little amplification to those who have studied the sixth and seventh grades of the Brotherhood College Work.

Thoth finds that time is angular in movement, yet being within curved walls and to penetrate into past time the consciousness must be moved in curves starting in the pineal, the same exercise given earlier.

Thoth mastered time and was able to move backward and forward in time seeing strange sights and learning from sight man's beginning.

Thoth again exhorts man to seek for light for only thus can they know their own soul. He also tells that in all matter light or consciousness exists though not always conscious consciousness.

Thoth tells of his wonderful experience in Amenti. When the Lords opened the path to their own cycles and allowed him to see with his own eyes that which exists beyond. From this Thoth learned that progression and order are the same in all cosmic cycles and that all are working in harmony toward the same ends.

Thoth was able to see the purpose behind the pushing out into space of Cosmic Cycles and with the Lord of Nine could feel the drawing together of the extensions of the different I. Yods. He learned that in words, which are examples of vibration lie the key to the opening of spaces and even cycles. He gives a vibratory word which is the Key of Life.

He speaks of interlocking worlds and spaces set apart from the one in which we dwell, each of these filled with manifestations of consciousness. He then relates a wonderful experience of calling from within the sixth dimension one who had been imprisoned by the Lords of Arulu.

She was one who, when we occupied the past Cosmic Cycle attempted to come into this cosmic cycle and failed and was imprisoned by the Lords of Arulu. Thoth through his knowledge opens the gateway and calls forth this imprisoned consciousness.

He commands the Lords to release her and by their secret names forces obedience. She then again becomes a part of this consciousness of which she once before was a part.

He states that knowledge is called by the ignorant, magic, and tells them not to be afraid for all is manifestation of law. Everyone has the force if he knows how to use it, but few have the knowledge.

Those who fear the unknown make of that fear a living thing. All fears of mankind have their source in the Dark Lords, conquer fear and be free. Man makes himself according to his thought a being of light or one of darkness.

TABLET XI

Thoth tells men of his time about the ages they and their ancestors have known him and this alone should have been enough to make them realize his power. He reminds them that he has been the keeper of the mysteries of past ages, and has brought them from savagery to light. He tells them that he is now going to reveal to them some of the elder mysteries revealed to him and his ancestors by the Children of Light and the Lords of the Cycles.

Thoth tells them how a way may be formed to open the gateway to the Halls of Amenti. Drawing a line in a geometrical angle from the Sphinx, the key to opening the secret chamber beneath the pyramid may be found.

The cycles Thoth speaks of are the cosmic cycles from the positive side of this Arech and the negative side of the other Arech toward which we are moving. The negative side of this and the positive side of the other, each have fourteen cosmic cycles. The Lords of the Cycles are of the central all of each cosmic consciousness. They know the eventual perfection of all.

For the first time Thoth mentions the Lord from below, i.e. the Lower cosmic cycle. Each cosmic consciousness thus has its representative in all cosmic cycles.

Thoth is told by the Lord of Nine that though he is great and one with the cosmic consciousness, yet there are mysteries of which he, as yet, does not know.

Thoth is told that though he knows much, yet hidden

within each cosmic consciousness are things he will not fully know until all become one.

The expansion of each consciousness is different for each is performing a different part in the infinite plan. Each supplements the other so that the growth of each one reacts upon the other. One is just as necessary as the other though some can perform greater tasks.

There is no real above or below for these are comparative terms.

The cosmic consciousnesses are the means through which the Torch Bearer changes disorder and chaos to order and law. Each works in its own space fulfilling necessary functions and the lower cosmic cycle is just as important in the great plan as the highest. The higher cosmic cycles are merely of greater ability. All cosmic consciousnesses are one in the final analysis just as all units of soul are one in the cosmic consciousness.

The difference in ability of the higher and lower cosmic consciousnesses is compared to the boy and man. Thoth is truly giving an example of the Microcosm and Macrocosm, as above so below.

The Lords though manifesting in Amenti, are yet connected with and a part of their own cosmic cycle. Their purpose in manifesting in Cosmic Cycles other than their own is for the purpose of aiding certain growths in the soul of man, and transmitting the results to their own cosmic consciousness, thus laying the foundation for the quality of the disorder allowed to flow to each Cosmic Cycle.

Perfection would be the goal though we should always realize that perfection is proceeding in direct proportion to our own growth.

What today seems perfection, tomorrow will be imperfection for we know that perfection is not yet realized, even in the Torch Bearer.

Thoth says that now he goes to Amenti, yet will live with them in the truth he has taught, almost the same as the sayings of Jesus. He gives the injunctions for them to turn all effort toward becoming one with the light.

Thoth concludes the tablet with the command to lift their eyes to the Sun and break free from darkness.

TABLET XII

Thoth has conquered time and therefore has full realization of the law of cause and effect. He has been able to penetrate to past and effect back to cause and know that nothing happens by chance and that the future is not fixed by fate, but reached by the law of effect resulting from cause set up. From the first cause to the fartherest extension all things must move according to this law. Knowing this man should be careful of the causes he sets up.

Thoth begins to speak of the future according to causes set up.

Man's destiny is the final blending with light even though he moves through darkness during material incarnations. When he speaks of the future light-born he is speaking of the seventh cycle and he also tells of the chaos that must come first, though in the end light will conquer the darkness.

Man has risen high in development in past ages and passed on closer to the Sun state and what has happened before will happen again. The ones to whom Thoth spoke would overcome and pass on, their place to be taken by another wave of consciousness from a lower planet.

The ancient race would in time be forgotten and the rulers would become Gods to those who came after; of such were Osiris, Horus and Isis.

Man's soul only remains on this planet until he receives the first degree of illumination, then passes to

Venus, from there to Mercury and finally to the Sun where it becomes one with the cosmic consciousness.

After they are gone the knowledge they have will be forgotten by man, excepting those who are appointed custodians. The age old struggle will go on, man constantly striving to regain that which he lost. Some there are who are so greatly in disorder that they will strive to hold others back, but light must conquer darkness, order banish disorder, though the earth tremble from the combat.

According to the prophecy the time is now when this shall come to pass.

The prophecy on this page is so plain no comment is needed save to say that we are now entering on the period spoken of.

In the end light will reign and man becomes one with the all pervading consciousness and shall pass as one into the higher cosmic cycle.

Thoth prepared to leave the outer earth and return to Amenti, placing his body beneath the Fire of Life, while his soul goes elsewhere. When man again rises to light, he promises that he will come forth again.

He adjures them to guard the secrets he has given them and especially the entrance to the Halls of Amenti. How well they kept their trust is shown by the fact that it is still guarded by their descendants.

TABLET XIII

Thoth promised to teach the secret of the Flower of Life and when they attain oneness they shall go to Amenti.

The Flower of Life is the solar-plexus of earth and from it spirit flows holding earth in form.

The same spirit is in man as in earth, only different in quantity.

Man is dual in polarity and when one pole becomes unbalanced the equilibrium of the body is shaken and sickness and death appear. Perfect balancing of the polarities eliminates sickness and disease.

The Flower of Life exerts a balancing effect on the polarities of the body, holding them in even equilibrium.

The rest of this tablet is so plain it needs no interpretation, for only definite exercises are given.

SUPPLEMENTARY TABLETS 11 & 12

TABLET XI

List ye, O Man, to the deep hidden wisdom, lost to the world since the time of the Dwellers, lost and forgotten by men of this age.

Know ye this earth is but a portal, guarded by powers unknown to man. Yet, the Dark Lords hide the entrance that leads to the Heaven born land. Know ye, the way to the sphere of Arulu is guarded by barriers, opened only to light-born man.

Upon earth I am the holder of the keys to the gates of the Sacred Land. Commanded I, by the powers beyond me, to leave the keys to the world of man. Before I depart I give ye the Secrets of how ye may rise from the bondage of darkness, cast off the fetters of flesh that have bound ye, rise from the darkness into the Light. Know ye, the Soul must be cleansed of its darkness, ere ye may enter the portals of light. Thus I establish among ye the Mysteries so that the Secrets may always be found. Aye, though men may fall into darkness, always the light will shine as a guide, hidden in darkness, veiled in symbols, always the way to the portal will be found. Man in the future will deny the mysteries, but always the way the seeker will find.

Now I command ye to maintain my secrets, giving only to those ye have tested, so that the pure may not be corrupted so that the power of Truth may prevail.

List ye now to the unveiling of Mystery, list to the

symbols of Mystery I give. Make of it a religion, for only thus will its essence remain.

Regions there are two between this life and the Great One, travelled by the Souls who depart from this earth. Duat, the home of the powers of illusion, Sekhet Hetspet, the house of the Gods, Osiris, the symbol of the guard of the portal, who turns back the souls of unworthy men. Beyond lies the sphere of the heaven born powers, Arulu, the land where the Great Ones have passed. There, when my work among men has been finished, will I join the Great Ones of my Ancient home.

Seven are the mansions of the house of the Mighty, three guards the portal of each house from the darkness, fifteen the ways that lead to Duat, Twelve are the houses of the Lords of Illusion, facing four ways, each of them different. Forty and two are the great powers, judging the Dead who seek for the portal. Four are the Sons of Horus, two are the Guards of East and West—Isis, the mother who pleads for her children, Queen of the moon, reflecting the Sun. Ba is the Essence, living forever, Ka is the Shadow that man knows as life. Ba cometh not until Ka is incarnate. These are mysteries to preserve through the ages. Keys are they of life and of Death. Hear ye now the mystery of mysteries, learn of the circle beginningless and endless, the form of He who is one and in all. Listen and hear it, go forth and apply it, thus will ye travel the way that I go. Mystery in Mystery, yet clear to the Lightborn, the Secret of all I now will reveal. I will declare a secret to the initiated but let the door be wholly shut against the profane.

Three is the mystery, come from the great one, hear, and light on thee will dawn.

In the primeval dwell three unities, other than these none can exist. These are the equilibrium, source of creation, one God, one Truth, one point of freedom.

Three come forth from the three of the balance, all life, all good, all power.

Three are the qualities of God in his light-home—Infinite power, Infinite wisdom, Infinite Love.

Three are the powers given to the Masters—To transmute evil, assist good, use discrimination.

Three are the things inevitable for God to perform—Manifest power, wisdom and love.

Three are the powers creating all things—Divine Love possessed of perfect knowledge, Divine Wisdom knowing all possible means, Divine Power possessed by the joint will of Divine Love and Wisdom.

Three are the circles (or states) of existence: the circle of light where dwells nothing but God, and only the God can traverse it, the circle of chaos where all things by nature arise from death, the circle of awareness where all things spring from life.

All things animate are of three states of existence, chaos or death, liberty in humanity and felicity of Heaven.

Three necessities control all things, beginning in the Great Deep, the circle of chaos, plenituded in Heaven.

Three are the paths of the Soul—Man, Liberty, Light.

Three are the hindrances—lack of endeavor to obtain knowledge, non-attachment to God, attachment to evil. In man the three are manifest, three are the Kings of power within, three are the chambers of the mysteries, found yet not found in the body of man.

Hear ye now of he who is liberated, freed from the bondage of life into light. Knowing the source of all worlds shall be open,—aye even the Gates of Arulu shall not be barred. Yet heed, O Man, who wouldst enter heaven. If ye be not worthy better would it be to fall into the fire: know ye the Celestials pass through the pure flame at every revolution of the heavens, they bathe in the fountains of light.

List ye O Man to this mystery—long in the past before ye were man-born I dwelled in Ancient Atlantis. There in the Temple I drank of the wisdom, poured as a fountain of light from the Dweller. Give the key to ascend to the Presence of Light in the Great world. Stood I before the Holy (one) enthroned in the flower of fire, veiled was he by the lightnings of darkness, else my Soul by the Glory have been shattered.

Forth from the feet of his Throne like the diamond, rolled forth four rivers of flame from his foot-stool, rolled through the channels of clouds to the Man-world. Filled was the hall with Spirits of Heaven; wonder of wonders was the Starry palace—above the sky like a rainbow of Fire and Sunlight were formed the spirits, sang they the glories of the Holy One. Then from the midst of the Fire came a voice, "Behold the Glory of the First Cause." I beheld that light, high above all darkness, reflected in my own being. I attained, as it were, to the God of all Gods, the Spirit-Sun, the Sovereign of the Sun spheres.

Again came the Voice. "There is one, even the First, who hath no beginning, who hath no end; who hath made all things—who governs all, who is good, who is just, who illumines, who sustains."

Then from the throne there poured a great radiance, surrounding and lifting my soul by its power. Swiftly I moved through the spaces of Heaven, shown was I the mystery of mysteries, shown the Secret heart of the cosmos. Carried was I to the land of Arulu, stood before the Lords in their Houses—opened they the Doorway so I might glimpse the primeval chaos. Shuddered my soul to the vision of horror, shrank back my soul from the ocean of darkness. Then saw I the need for the barriers, saw the need for the Lords of Arulu. Only they with their Infinite balance could stand in the way of the inpouring chaos, only they could guard God's creation.

Then did I pass round the circle of eight, saw all the souls who had conquered the darkness, saw the splendor of light where they dwelled. Longed I to take my place in their circle, but longed I also for the way I had chosen, when I stood in the Halls of Amenti and made my choice of the work I would do.

Passed I from the Halls of Arulu down to the earth space where my body lay. Arose I from the earth where I rested. Stood I before the Dweller, gave my pledge to renounce my Great Right until my work on earth was completed. Until the Age of darkness be past.

List ye, O man, to the words I shall give ye—in them shall ye find the Essence of Life. Before I return to the Halls of Amenti, taught shall ye be the Secrets of Secrets, how ye too may arise to the light. Preserve them and guard them, hide them in symbols, so the profane will laugh and renounce. In every land form ye the mysteries, make the way hard for the seeker to tread. Thus will the weak and the wavering be rejected, thus will the secrets be hidden and guarded, held till the time when the wheel shall be turned.

Through the dark ages, waiting and watching, my Spirit shall remain in the deep hidden land. When one has passed all the trials of the outer, summon ye me by the Key that ye hold. Then will I, the Initiator answer, come from the Halls of the Gods in Amenti. Then will I receive the initiate, give him the words of power.

Hark ye, remember, these words of warning, bring not to me one lacking in wisdom, impure in heart or weak in his purpose, else I will withdraw from ye your power to summon me from the place of my sleeping.

Go forth and conquer the element of darkness—exalt in thy nature thine essence of light.

Now go ye forth and summon thy brothers so that I may impart the wisdom to light thy path when my presence is gone. Come to the chamber beneath my temple, eat not of food until three days are past. There will I give thee the essence of wisdom so that with power ye may shine amongst men. There will I give unto thee the secrets so that ye too may rise to the Heavens—God-men in Truth as in essence ye be. Depart now and leave me while I summon those ye know of but as yet know not.

TABLET XII

SECRET OF SECRETS

Now ye assemble my children, waiting to hear the Secret of Secrets, which shall give ye power to unfold the God-man, give ye the way to Eternal Life. Plainly shall I speak the Unveiled Mysteries, no dark sayings shall I give unto thee. Open thine ears now my children, hear and obey the words that I give.

First I shall speak of the fetter of darkness which bind ye in chains to the sphere of the earth.

Darkness and Light are both of one nature, different only in seeming, for each arose from the source of all. Darkness is disorder, light is order; Darkness transmuted is light of the light. This, my children, your purpose in being, transmutation of darkness to light.

Hear ye now of the mystery of nature, the relations of life to the earth where it dwells. Know ye, ye are threefold in nature, physical, astral and mental in one. Three are the qualities of each of the natures, nine in all, as above, so below.

In the physical are these channels, the blood which moves in vortical motion, reacting on the heart to continue its beating. Magnetism which moves through the nerve paths, carrier of energies to all cells and tissues. Akasa which flows through channels, subtle yet physical, completing the channels. Each of the three attuned with each other, each affecting the life of the body. Form they the Skeletal framework through which the subtle ether flows. In their mastery lies the Secret of Life in the body. Relinquished only by will of the adept, when his purpose in living is done.

Three are the natures of the Astral, mediator it between above and below—not of the physical, not of the Spiritual, but able to move above and below.

Three are the natures of Mind, carrier it of the Will of the Great One. Arbitrator of Cause and Effect in thy life. Thus is formed the threefold being, directed from above by the power of four. Above and beyond man's threefold nature lies the realm of the Spiritual Self. Four is it in qualities, shining in each of the planes of existence, but thirteen in one, the mystical number. Based on the qualities of man are the Brothers, each shall direct the unfoldment of being, each shall channels be of the Great One.

On earth man is in bondage, bound by space and time to the earth plane. Encircling each planet a wave of vibration, binds him to his plane of unfoldment. Yet within man is the Key to releasement, within man may freedom be found.

When ye have released the self from the body, rise to the outermost bounds of your earth-plane, speak ye the word Dor-e-ul-la. Then for a time your light will be lifted, free may ye pass the barriers of space. For a time of half of the sun (six hours), free may ye pass the barriers of earth-plane, see and know those who are beyond thee—yea, to the highest worlds may ye pass. See your own possible heights of unfoldment, know all earthly futures of Soul.

Bound are ye in your body, but by the power ye may be free. This is the Secret whereby bondage shall be replaced by freedom for thee.

Calm let thy mind be, at rest be thy body—conscious only of freedom from flesh. Center thy being on the goal of thy longing, think over and over that thou wouldst be free. Think of this word—La-um-I-l-gan, over and over in thy mind let it sound. Drift with the sound to the place of thy longing, free from the bondage of flesh by thy will.

Hear ye while I give the greatest of secrets—how ye may enter the Halls of Amenti, enter the place of the immortals as I did, stand before the Lords in their places.

Lie ye down in rest of thy body, calm thy mind so no thought disturbs thee. Pure must ye be in mind and in purpose, else only failure will come unto thee. Vision Amenti as I have told in my Tablets. Long with fullness of heart to be there. Stand before the Lords in thy mind's eye. Pronounce the words of power I give—Mekut-el-shab-el hale-zur-ben-el-zabrut Zin-efrim—Quar-el (Mentally). Relax thy mind and thy body—then be sure your soul will be called.

Now give I the Key to Shamballa—the place where my Brothers live in the darkness. Darkness but filled with light of the Sun—Darkness of Earth, but light of the Spirit, guides for ye when my day is done.

Leave thou thy body as I have taught thee. Pass to the barriers of the deep, hidden place. Stand before the gates and their guardians, command thy entrance by these words—"I am the Light, In me is no darkness, Free am I of the bondage of night, open thou the way of the twelve and the one, so I may pass to the realm of wisdom." When they refuse thee, as surely they will; command them to open by these words of power, "I am the light, for me are no barriers, open I command by the Secret of Secrets—Edom-el-ahim-Sabbert-Zur—adom." Then if thy words have been "Truth" of the highest, open for thee the barriers will fall.

Now, I leave thee my children, down, yet up, to the Halls shall I go. Win ye the way to me, my children, truly my brothers shall ye become.

Thus finish I my writings—Keys let them be to those who come after, but only to those who seek my wisdom, for only for these am I the Key and the Way.

ATLANTIS AND ITS PART IN THE NEW AGE

BY DR. DOREAL

It may seem strange to some of you that we should connect Atlantis with the new and greater age which is to
appear just around the corner but if we know anything about
occult traditions concerning Atlantis we can see that there is
a very important relationship between Atlantis and the New
Age because at the very height of its glory Atlantis was in
almost every respect just what we will find in the New Age
and when I say, "In almost every respect," I mean, materially
speaking and spiritually speaking so far as concerns, the
evolvement and evolution of consciousness. It is true that the
Atlanteans were far different in physical structure from what
the finally perfected man will be. Yet, their civilization at the
height of their advancement was so great that what we call
civilization today would seem like that of the most uncivilized race of savages on earth today in comparison. That may
seem like a very strong statement to make. Yet, if we realize
that the Atlanteans had learned to do away with all the complicated machinery, that utilized steam and electrical power
and even atomic power that we have today and are just learning about and that they had learned to utilize the subtle forces
of Nature in the ether in practically everything they did, that
they had evolved a system of government that was almost
completely perfect, that they had learned to place the ideals,
the philosophy, the seeking for God above everything else
that existed in the world, we can understand why there is a

great relationship between Atlantis and the New Age.

In this I am going to give you some illustrations of Atlantis and the life in Atlantis so that you can get some glimmering at least of the things that lie before us.

Some people will say, "But Atlantis is mythological. We have no written records of Atlantis. There are no books about Atlantis excepting those written by men in our modern times. There are no records of that civilization, if civilization it was, excepting by Plato and one or two others. There are no contemporary records of Atlantis and its advancements excepting in folklore, and mythology." My answer to that is very simple, that it has become a proven fact that prehistory is almost always recorded in the mythology and folklore of peoples. By study of folklore and mythology it is possible to learn a great many things about ancient races and civilizations that have become completely lost by what we call practical historians, that we can learn a great deal about the ancient cultures and about the people that lived far beyond the dawn of recorded history.

We know that according to Plato and the records he had access to, the sinking of Atlantis occurred 12,000 years before his time. Yet, geology and other evidence shows us that it must have been at least four times since the sinking of that land mass once occupied the Atlantic Ocean. As a matter of fact, the Atlantic Ocean derived its name from Atlantis.

In some of the early priestly accounts Atlantis is mentioned, and we also know that there has been discovered in the past few years a tremendous amount of factual evidence to prove the existence of such a land mass. I am using the term, 'land mass' instead of saying, 'island' or continent,—however, the oldest records say, 'islands'. I am speaking literally from the historical standpoint. For instance, we know that the Mayans themselves were not Atlanteans but that their culture and knowledge of archaeology, of the stars and of mathematics had been taught them by people who had come somewhere from the Atlanteans. That we have learned because there has been some deciphering of early Mayan records.

Most of you, I imagine, have heard of LePlongeon because he wrote a number of books concerning the Mayas, Queen Moo and The Egyptian Sphinx. Then there is one called, "Queen Moo's Talisman". Actually, I do not think he correctly translated many of them. Nevertheless, he was the pioneer in that field. A great difficulty that we run into is when the Spaniards conquered the Mayas. Today, there are only six known Mayan codexes or books and peculiarly enough one of those is written in the Greek alphabet. I mean that every letter of the Greek alphabet is found in it in the form of a poem which translated tells of the sinking of the mother land, cities being drowned and people finally leaving and migrating to other places so there is also a number of other evidence.

I was looking at an old National Geographic sometime ago and it showed a stone and over it was a little subtitle, "This stone is from Atlantis." It did not make any explanation but that "This stone is from Atlantis." We know also that Egypt had the legend that their country had been settled by Atlanteans. We have considerable evidence that ancient Iran was once a colony of ancient Atlantis. As a matter of fact, there is all the difference in the world between mythology and fairy tales. A myth tells in story form, sometimes highly exaggerated things which sometimes appear fantastic but after a while you begin to find there are certain common factors that run throughout all of them and then another factor and after awhile you have a picture and finally, you come out with something you can lay your hands on. That is one reason I have collected around 800 volumes of folklore and mythology. I have not done so because I need that to prove that Atlantis existed but merely what I like to discover the factual things that remain to us in story form. It is like the Old Testament; some parts are factual, some are mythological but the mythological ones do carry an account of some belief, some tradition that the Jewish people once had.

Now coming down to Atlantis: Atlantis sank approximately fifty thousand years ago. That was the time when the deluge or flood that we read about in the Bible took place. Whether we believe it or not the Biblical account of the flood or of Noah was one, not of Jewish or Hebrew origin but they borrowed like the Jews of Egypt did when they left Egypt, from the Chaldeans. The Chaldeans had many legends and they were embodied in books formed of clay. They were bound after the particular characters had been inscribed on them and the Chaldean accounts tell of the deluge and in different form of course from the Jewish account in the Old Testament but after all they took the story and placed it around their own culture.

The Chaldeans said that long, long ago, at a period they placed at about fifty thousand years ago, they said that the

Gods looked down at earth and saw man had become evil. He had become proud. His cities reached into the sky. He gained great knowledge and great wisdom but he had lost his respect for the Gods so the Gods met at a council and they tried to destroy man by water but one of the Gods, Ea, the God of the water, the God of the sea or ocean had one man that he loved. This man had always been a very good man, one of the very few and Ea wanted to tell this man so he could save himself but the Gods themselves promised they would not tell it to any living man so Ea whispered it to the reeds and as this man was walking through the reeds, the reeds whispered it to the man and told him what to do to save himself so he built a great ark and into it he took animals two by two and his sons and daughters and when the water came and drowned the earth he was saved. That story was old in Chaldea before the period set in the Old Testament for the deluge. They came along, put Noah in it and said it was one of their ancestors that did it which is alright but that just shows you how stories grow and become started. I do not doubt that the Chaldeans got the story from somebody else, maybe the people of the sea and nobody knows who they were, where they came from or anything about them.

I have a very unusual statue that no one has ever seen anything like. It shows two figures standing on the bank with water proceeding from it after the deluge, holding the Kraakon, the God of space.

That story unquestionably originated as did that of the story of the deluge among the peoples of all the widely scattered lands of earth, in the sinking of Atlantis because with such a vast area of land as comprised Atlantis there had to be a various sinking of land, and raising of others. That always rather amused me when we read in the Bible—I am sorry but I do not believe the Bible from cover to cover. A lot of the old things in the Old Testament are myth. It shows when the deluge came and only Noah and his daughters were safe and I read in the Chaldean records, where a war was fought sixty years after the deluge in which three million men took part. I will be doggoned if I believe Noah had three million grandsons in sixty years. In other words, the story basically may be true but the time element is out of balance and that is the way of many things. We have to study contemporary history as well as mythology to find out whether things are in proper sequence.

Atlantis sank about fifty thousand years ago. At that time, the time of the sinking, scattered over the face of the earth there were numerous tribes of barbarous and savage men. Only on two continents, or rather on two land masses—one a continent, one a group of large islands, some very large, there were two great civilized nations: the Lemurians and the Atlanteans. All the rest of the world, with the exception of a few scattered colonies that had been established in different parts of the world, the entire world was composed of savage and barbarous races and tribes. Unquestionably, most of the people of earth today, there are exceptions of course, are descended from savage and barbarous tribes that were left after the deluge, because after the deluge there were only comparatively few Atlanteans left, though it is true the Atlantean strain has come down through the ages almost pure into the present time. Yet, such are very, very rare. I think that in an entire life I have met two persons that were descended without a break on both sides from the original families that were left after the deluge. It may be of interest to you to know that all the Atlanteans know each other.

Even at the time of the sinking of Atlantis there was a great degeneration of the Atlanteans. Now the Atlanteans came into being as a nation or nations some five hundred thousand years before its sinking. When I say, "came into being as a nation,"—I mean that before that time, the ancestors who became the Atlanteans were in themselves in a comparatively uncivilized and savage state, very little more advanced than the people are here in America today and will anybody deny that people are uncivilized and savages today with two wars and getting all ready to do it again. Do you call that civilization? Nothing was ever settled by wars. People have to learn that there are other ways of doing things than by force. That is the first beginning of civilization in the individual or the nation, when they learn that there are many ways of doing things than by force. When warring nations are living side by side with one civilized nation has to learn to protect itself. The Atlanteans knew how to do that. I wish the people in the world today knew as much about it as the Atlanteans.

The prehistoric Atlanteans came into a group of islands, very large islands, even the smallest, that afterwards became known as Atlantis, a time of approximately five hundred thousand years before its sinking, when they came into the Atlantean Islands they found them inhabited by a race of people that were not human and yet, I use the term, 'people' advisedly because they had intelligence; they had knowledge, mental powers surpassing the people of their time and certainly, the people of this present time. Those people had physically evolved in a line of evolution different from that of human kind. They had evoluted from the serpent who walked upright like a man. When the Atlanteans fought the Serpent People they had a very hard time in their battle with them. The Serpent People desperately fought against the invaders. The Atlanteans who came in were not all of the same race. They were of various races who had joined together in combination or union. They had learned to form a permanent union of cooperation of a group of scattered nations and races and the original Atlanteans were of a different number of races. There were the Red Race. The copper skinned race is not derived entirely from the Red Atlantean Race. There was a White Race; there was a Yellow race and Gold race. I might mention just in passing that the Osage Indian Tribe was from, that is, its parent stock was formed from an admixture of the Yellow, Gold and one of the prehistoric savage races. That is, of course, after the sinking of Atlantis and the Osage Indians still have definite characteristics of those races. There was also a Black race, not the Negro race. They had straight hair, very finely cut features and were in no way related to the common so-called Negro race and there also were two races that have no counterpart on earth today. There was a Blue race and a Green race. All of those took part in the original invasion and taking of the Atlantean Island group and fought the Serpent people. That is one reason, in the legends of every land and nation we find stories of the Serpent race that contended with mankind in his beginning because so far as even our legendary history goes it only goes back to the Atlantean Age.

In certain islands in the Pacific the culture and remnants of the most ancient races are under the ocean. They fought the Serpent people and these Serpent people walked upright like a man. They had a body covered with fine scales and their head was like that of a tremendously great snake and their mouth was just about that wide and they had a certain mental power that the race of man did not have at that time and does not have today except in a few isolated instances. That was hypnotic power. They could assume the form of anything they could cast a hypnotic spell on and then the serpent struck.

That is the reason even that statement in the Bible, "and woman was given the power to bruise the Serpent's head with her heel," and the serpent who tempted man in the Garden of Eden. Adam and Eve became a symbol of mankind and Adam and Lileth became the symbol of the tempter and Adam married Eve and was tempted by Lileth and Lileth was the first wife of Adam. That is left out of the Bible but is found in Jewish legends.

After the passing of many centuries those who became Atlanteans were firmly settled and they had killed out the majority of the Serpent people but there were still a few hundred of them that lived and they lived and they injected themselves into various places and they remained hidden through long periods of ages but they did form an underground that constantly fought against the advancement of Atlantis.

Atlantis became very great mentally and spiritually and shall we say, occultly speaking, because they learned to utilize all the powers of the etheric currents and etheric forces so they used them not just in occult practices but in their everyday life. To give you an example: they learned how to build without hands. I have sometimes wondered if in spite of the stories in the Bible of all the gold and wood and things Solomon put in his temple, if Solomon had not learned or found one of the etheric producing machines of Atlantis and built his temple without the sound of hammer. I have always been rather curious about that and to satisfy my curiosity I went back in time to the time of the building Solomon's Temple and I found sure enough, he had discovered one of the Atlantean building machines and that he started in to use it. He built a model of his temple, turned on the power, turned on the power wrong and it did not build but he still had a vision, a dream and then went ahead and built the temple after the model he had found of this machine.

Let me describe that machine to you as simply as I can. They did not have to build their temples or houses, not with metals or wood or stone or even with their hands. The only workshops that the Atlanteans had was workshops of producing miniatures, a few factories where they would turn out in miniature, little figures of everything they wanted. If they were going to build a city they would pick out a site, then construct in miniature all the things they wanted for it, using gold, silver, wood, or whatever it might be. Then that was placed in a certain machine they had. Then two crystals were focused on the point they wanted that building to appear. It would not build beyond a certain range or point but they would focus that on a certain point. The miniature was in a certain chamber and then the operator who was one that was specially trained, one of the guild of builders would seat himself before that machine, he would pour into it a certain mental impulse and he would cause to flow, through his body, and through that machine a stream of certain etheric currents.

There were and are twelve basic etheric energies or currents and in Atlantis the men were all, and some women, organized into guilds, not like our modern labor unions but in guilds and each one because of certain peculiar qualities they had was able to control the flow of one of these twelve subdivisions of etheric currents more completely than any other person. The guild of builders, for instance, all those people were born under a certain sign and could control those powers better than anyone else. They started that flowing, then this machine which was simply a series of coils built around a central coil formed of two metals, one red and one kind of a silvery-gray in color, natural metals found in Atlantis, but not known on earth today, though at one time the Grand Gallery of the Great Pyramid was lined with those two metals. Through a series of coils and these coils were not formed of wire. I mention that in case you try to wire a coil. These themselves had been built by another guild. Those coils were coils of energy. They built energy patterns or webs that remained static in their place and they knew so much about the forces of Nature they were able to build a force shield and maintain it around. Now when this current poured through it also poured through these coils and sent it into the facsimile which was projected and they were centered at one point and where those beams came to a focal point a building grew in exact facsimile of the miniature and it grew in proportion to the dimensions that had been embodied in the miniature.

If the miniature was one-fourth of an inch high and one-half inch long, they could estimate the size of the rooms or building so building of an Atlantean city was no arduous task. In the later days the only Atlantean city that had been built by hands was one where the priestly class and philosopher class met because that was the first city built on Atlantean Islands and it was kept more as the form of a museum of antiquity than anything else, but the same was true of everything that they did, all the things they did, when they made their ships that would fly through the air, etc., they were all made in the same manner.

A moment ago I told about how and why they were divided into twelve guilds—to explain that I have to explain something about the calendar system. They divided their years through twelve months of thirty days each and then, every fourth year, the one that was 29 had thirty days so they, actually had thirteen months instead of the twelve we have now. As a matter of fact, I don't know whether you realize it now but every so many hundred years we lose so much time. They learned this, that if a person was born under a particular sign and they had thirteen signs instead of twelve signs that we now have in the zodiac. They had thirteen signs, not twelve and the thirteen signs, each of them had a greater ability to manipulate certain of the etheric forces than the others. They could all manipulate all of them but some seemed to have a greater power because they were born under the same sign; I will not say related or attuned to that particular division of the etheric powers. I said there were twelve guilds so twelve of the signs which are familiar to our signs that we know now. As a matter of fact, astrology originated in Atlantis and later it became transformed, one sign was lost and we came to have twelve signs but the twelve signs could control these powers. There was a thirteenth sign, a controlling or directing sign and those born under that sign from the time of their birth were trained for coordinating and correlating all the others. When Atlantis sank and was destroyed the co-ordinators passed and there was no longer any use for that knowledge. It could not be utilized.

The Atlanteans had gained certain powers. They had gained the power to move through space, not through unlimited distances but they could move through space as far as the moon and for a time there were certain colonies established on the moon. They moved to the moon not through space ships but through a variation of the same ability that they built their buildings with. They could use that as a projector and where they focussed the rays from it, an object placed in a disintegrating chamber, reassembled at the point they were focussed. That was the common method of transportation in Atlantis at the height of its glory before it fell. There were few cars driven by subetheric energies that moved on the surface and quite a number of planes built according to the principle I have here. A long time ago they were propelled along magnetic currents and they were propelled along magnetic currents and they were able to move very fast, very rapidly. As a matter of fact if I am not mistaken, these flying disks that they have seen are a variation of those that the Atlanteans used.

I wonder if any of you read in the paper sometime ago about that ship those two airline pilots saw. It had two decks, with windows brilliantly lighted and shooting fire about forty feet and they were so blinded by the flare or light from it that they had to turn on their instrument lights, moving somewhere between five and seven hundred miles an hour and went right on up. If I am not mistaken we do not have to worry about that being a Russian ship. Some of our neighbors needed some material and came down and got it but they have been doing that for a long time. For a long time they have been coming down and getting things out of the sea but they did not want to bother us or let us know about it because we are too uncivilized.

There are marvelous things just at hand and we cannot see them because we are blinded by our own negation and it will be wonderful when we begin to see people begin to grow into their true estate. If they wanted to visit one of their friends on the other side of the city, they did not walk or ride because each house had one chamber in it that was fixed; another variation of the building instrument and of the projecting instrument for long distance travel. All they would have to do is set its dial on the number. Those for long distance projections were held in certain places and not open to the public but they had a system just like our telephone system. Dial a number and come out, in a chamber of the other, shall we say, telephone; a curious and easy method of transportation. Atlanteans knew some things we are just beginning to learn something about. They knew that the individual ego was not bound or hindered by the body and the human body itself was just a certain pattern held in form by certain forces. Disassociate its elements and the pattern then was projected along one etheric wave which would also carry the astral structure of the body. It had to carry two things: the astral structure and the physical pattern of the body. When a person passed that way their whole body actually was disintegrated into nothingness, but each pattern of these bodies was constantly pouring forth a stream of radiation which passed from one machine to another and arrived instantly. That pattern picked up the elements necessary, assembled them and there the body formed. Though they did not look any different yet, every time they went from place to place it was an entirely different body. Stepped down, that became the basis of one of the great discoveries of Atlantis. They learned this, that basically, the human body became diseased because there were certain destructions in the basic pattern of the human body and it would get this malignant growth or that disfunction or they would be afflicted with a broken bone or what have you so their medicine and system of healing eliminated the physical body entirely. They did not pay any attention to the physical body. They began to study the basic pattern. They learned to take the human body, perhaps something had gone wrong, perhaps some disease had started. The doctor would put them under a certain machine, something like the X-ray, excepting when they looked into it they did not see the skeleton. They looked through that and were able to see the flow of etheric currents that formed the body and they could see where there was a distortion in that pattern. Then they would manipulate them until they would straighten out the distorted physical pattern. Then they would put the person in a machine, transport them from one place to another and then they would leave out the disease pattern and reintegrate the elements and when they came out, they came out with the pattern that had been corrected.

A person once told me that every great natural healer (there are such things as great natural healers) that regardless of the methods used that the person is healed in time. Said that everyone of those persons, the healers, would by direction of consciousness and when they would heal would correct or straighten out the pattern in the body of the person they were healing, but in such a case, it took time, whereas, when the Atlanteans did it, they just blew them up here and reassembled them up here with a new body that matched the pattern. In other words, there was no such thing as a disease or sickness allowed to remain except for a short period of time in any person in Atlantis so the Atlanteans lived to a very great age. Thousands of years was nothing for Atlanteans to live. Finally, the physical body did die, not because they could not conquer disease but because the basic pattern would break down under certain poisonous emanations from the sun and when that happened, there was nothing they could do about that.

I might say this, that exactly those same things will be a part of the New Age is coming to us. In other words there will be no more sickness, no more disease and there will finally come a time when there will be no more death. When we read in the Bible about the men who lived to be about a thousand years old or four or five thousand years, there must have been something which enabled those men to live to those vast ages. Perhaps they were in contact with some of those raised descendents of those Atlantean continents, but unquestionably their knowledge and power exceeding anything that we even dream about today. That is the reason I say that they were civilized, because they did not fight among themselves. I am not talking about the last days of Atlantis.

They considered there was an over-Spirit which was the source of emanation and that the immaterial form covering the spiritual was beneath the material. That may sound like a peculiarly phrased statement. They believed in the magnetic principle, in universal creation, in the electrical principle but those were merely the basic or minor applications of force and power. They knew the power of the infinite mind manifested in time, space and light and they knew and used the developing principle in universal creation. They had early learned one basic fact, that nothing existed without an infinite center and that infinite center has its counterpart in the world of man. Therefore, they began early to seek the counterpart in man. They looked within from the very beginning instead of without for the source of their powers. They considered it to be very crude to have to use any form of material force or energy to bring about force for the things they wanted.

Sometimes, they built instruments but they used them only as a channel, because they had learned to tap the universal currents and tap them at will. There was no sickness and no disease and death was something they put off until practically, they were ready to pass anyway, but their bodies were still strong and they would walk into special places set aside for that purpose and break up their physical and die. When they had completed what they wanted to do and were ready to go on into a greater and higher thing they went. They were not afraid of death and put off their physical bodies at will.

They did not conceive there was such a thing as death and went through transition at will but not in the sense of committing suicide. They merely laid down one vehicle to pick up another and they carried on for a great time but they finally reached a point where all the souls that had originally inhabited Atlantis, had become so great spiritually speaking, that they no longer needed to incarnate in a physical body and passed, but those who passed had had children. For a long period of time the souls that came into the bodies of the children, had come from other planets, with souls that were lower in development, so low in fact, that though physically, they had inherited certain powers they did not have the spiritual evolution in harmony with it so they would and could use those powers constructively and so when that happened, the time came for them to pass and when those lesser souls that came after, people about like us or less, and when they began to use powers destructively, the Great Ones decided they must pass, so those physical powers could be taken away and they would reincarnate in places where the weapons they could use and the powers they had would be in accordance with their own particular evolvement at that time. Men had powers besides which the atom bomb is a child's firecracker, so the Great One and Ones decided that Atlantis should be destroyed, so they changed the balance of the earth and water rolled in, lands sank and other lands rose and Atlantis was destroyed but before they did that they had sent certain things to other lands, so those records were preserved, still are preserved, so those who have gone into the mysteries and permeated into the secret places have been able to see in operation as well as just the things they had. People say, "Why don't they give them to the world today?" Why should they give them to another world that is even less worthy? When we become ready the knowledge and powers will become ours and that time will be in the Golden Age. But that is the reason man must evolve spiritually. That is the reason we have to create the Golden Age within ourselves.

* * * * * * * * * * * *

BROTHERHOOD CHURCH & COLLEGE

The Brotherhood of the White Temple is a chartered Church, maintaining a College and other essential branches for the dissemination of Truth. The Brotherhood Church and the Brotherhood College function as two departments of teaching, each supporting the other. College Membership and Church Membership is interrelated and our students are members of both; for the Truth derived from the weekly lessons of both the College and Church help in the understanding of the other.

The Brotherhood is a corresponding Church and College. The College is a Metaphysical School wherein the Laws of the Universe are taught, and in which the student learns how to operate these Spiritual Laws through the exercise and initiations given him. The Church teaches all of the Mysteries taught by Jesus, the Christ, to his disciples. It teaches the student how to read the mystical writing found in the Bible and how to understand their true and concealed meaning. The members of the Church are shown how to attain citizenship in the coming Christ Kingdom, and how to become a perfect channel for the Divine Spirit.

Write for FREE Brochure, "Master of Destiny," describing the Teachings of the Brotherhood.

BROTHERHOOD OF THE WHITE TEMPLE
7830 OAK WAY
SEDALIA, COLORADO 80135
PHONE 303 688–3998
WEB SITE: www.bwtemple.org

Printed in the United States
70553LV00008B/34

9 781598 582420